William Denton

Montenegro

its people and their history

William Denton

Montenegro
its people and their history

ISBN/EAN: 9783337230647

Printed in Europe, USA, Canada, Australia, Japan

Cover: Foto ©Andreas Hilbeck / pixelio.de

More available books at **www.hansebooks.com**

MONTENEGRO

ITS PEOPLE AND THEIR HISTORY

BY THE REV. W. DENTON, M.A.
AUTHOR OF 'SERVIA AND THE SERVIANS,' 'THE CHRISTIANS OF TURKEY,'
ETC. ETC.

LONDON
DALDY, ISBISTER & CO.
56, LUDGATE HILL
1877

TO

NICHOLAS THE FIRST,

Prince of Montenegro and the Berda,

A BRAVE SOLDIER, A PATRIOT PRINCE,

AND

A CHRISTIAN GENTLEMAN.

PREFACE.

I owe it to the courtesy of the proprietors of the *Church Quarterly Review* that I have been able to embody in this small volume the greater part of an article on 'Montenegro,' contributed by me, in October last, to that periodical. By the like permission on the part of the publishers of *Good Words*, I have also made use of two papers written by me a few years since, and printed in that periodical. For the information contained in these papers and in the present volume I am indebted to my own observations made whilst travelling in Montenegro, to replies sent me in answer to inquiries made with a view to publication, and to such books as I believe may be depended upon for their accuracy. The information so obtained I have sought fairly to place before the reader; and that I may enable him to verify any statements made by me, I have cited my authorities throughout. I have made full use of the testimony and the language of others, because I prefer to use their words rather than my own. I have, so far as I could, avoided all questions of momentary political strife, believing that whatever may be thought of the present aspect of the Eastern question, most persons, be their party predilections what they may, will sympathize with the Montenegrins in their heroic struggle for independence and freedom of religious worship. In addition to the description of the physical aspect of the country and the institutions of its people, I have given a brief sketch of the history of Montenegro, which, without possessing any claim to research, will be, I imagine, new to most readers. But though I have sought to avoid all allusion to mere party politics, politics themselves it were impossible to avoid, even if I wished to do so, since politics is only another name for the history of the present.

22, WESTBOURNE SQUARE,
  May, 1877.

CONTENTS.

INTRODUCTION . . . .

PART I.
COUNTRY AND PEOPLE OF MONTENEGRO.

CHAPTER

I.—NAME—BOUNDARIES—SUPERFICIAL EXTENT—PASS FROM CATTARO 9

II.—RIVERS—MOUNTAINS—GEOLOGY OF MONTENEGRO—MOUNT LOVCHEN 21

III.—CLIMATE—PRODUCTION—EXPORTS AND IMPORTS—ROADS 38

IV.—POLITICAL DIVISIONS—CETINJE—NIEGUSH—RJEKA—DIOCLEA—OSTROG 52

V.—POPULATION—MILITARY FORCES—TACTICS . . 79

VI.—PRESENT MILITARY ORGANIZATION . . . 93

VII.—PHYSICAL CHARACTERS—LONGEVITY—DRESS—COTTAGES—HOME LIFE 103

VIII.—MORAL CHARACTERISTICS—POSITION OF WOMEN—HONESTY—CHASTITY—COURT OF APPEAL—CODE OF LAWS—EQUALITY OF PEOPLE . . 119

IX.—OCCUPATIONS—LAND TENURE—OFFICES—INCOME—EXPENDITURE 141

X.—LANGUAGE—LITERATURE—PRINTING PRESS . . 151

XI.—ECCLESIASTICAL STATE—EDUCATION . . . 161

PART II.

HISTORY OF MONTENEGRO.

CHAPTER	PAGE
XII.—Montenegrin History until the Battle of Kossova	179
XIII.—Montenegro an Independent Principality (1389—1516)	189
XIV.—The Legend of Stanicha	200
XV.—Montenegro under the Prince-Bishops: Period the First, Elective Bishops (A.D. 1516—1696)	210
XVI.—Hereditary Prince-Bishops—Danilo Petrovic	225
XVII.—The Vladikas Sava and Vassali (A.D. 1735—1782)	237
XVIII.—Peter I. (1782—1830.)	249
XIX.—Peter II. (1830—1851)	264
XX.—Restoration of the Secular Rule—Danilo II.	274
XXI.—Nicholas I. (1860)	288

INTRODUCTION.

THE war which has just broken out between Turkey and Russia, and which may yet involve at least some of the other powers of Europe in the struggle to obtain a better government for the long oppressed Christian subjects of Turkey, has made Montenegro a household word in this country. As this small Principality is but little known to Englishmen, and as it has now acquired an importance wholly incommensurate with its size and with the number of its inhabitants, it is my purpose to give, in part from notes made during a short visit to that country, in part from materials collected for this purpose, a brief account of the territory and people of Montenegro, together with an outline of the history of the Principality.

Apart from its share in the present war with Turkey, Montenegro, however, though the 'smallest among peoples,'* deserves our respect for the successful efforts it has made for the preservation of its independence, and may fairly claim a portion of that gratitude which we owe to the memory of John Sobieski and of the conquerors at Lepanto. A larger share, indeed, than they; since this small handful of mountaineers has struggled for four centuries with hardly any intermission against the Ottoman power, has never submitted to its yoke, has kept alive the hope of freedom in the Serb provinces on the south of the Danube, has beaten back the forces of Turkey even when in the full career of victory, and has thus served, often at the most critical moments of European history, as a breakwater against the inundation which once threatened to sweep away all vestiges of civilisation, of freedom, and of Christianity from the face of Europe. In short, for long years and centuries the whole life of the people of Montenegro was one prolonged fight of Marathon or Morgarten: one long unbroken struggle against the assaults of the most cruel and faithless of enemies, the common foe of the religion and the civilisation of Europe.' †

Another fact in the history of this people is equally deserving of our respect and admiration. Monte-

* TENNYSON.   † FREEMAN.

negro has not only offered at all times a ready asylum to the suffering subjects of the Ottoman Government, without distinction of race or creed, but so sacred is this right of asylum regarded by them, and so great is the confidence of their enemies in their chivalrous character, that during the wars along the frontier Mussulman women and children have frequently sought and found a haven of safety, not at a distance from but in the midst of their foes, and have lived without molestation among the Montenegrins, whilst these people were engaged in a fierce struggle for their existence with the brothers and husbands of the fugitives.* In striking distinction from the practice of their enemies, female honour and life and the helplessness of childhood have been always respected by them.

To recount our obligation, and the obligation of all Christendom, to this small state is to acknowledge the difficulties which lie in the way of any one who may attempt to give even an outline of the history of the Montenegrins. Their life is one

* In the early part of the present war Turkish women and children were received by the Montenegrins, and fed and lodged with the same care as the Christian fugitives from the Herzegovina. In October, 1875, the official returns give a list of fifty-two Turkish women and children who were at that moment receiving shelter within the Principality.

of primitive, and but for the warfare to which they have been compelled of almost arcadian, simplicity. Their history is one long epic, in which the deeds of heroism, wrought out in their mountain home, seems more fitted for the verse of the poet than for the sober pen of the historian. It is, indeed, hardly possible to relate the fortunes of this heroic people without appearing to encroach upon the province of the writers of romance, and thus 'begetting in the mind of the reader a restless suspicion of exaggeration and of fable.'* It is impossible that it should be otherwise. The fact that a state which makes but a mere speck on the map of Europe, with a population at the most of about thirty thousand men, women, and children,† should at the time when the Sultans of Turkey were most powerful and most bent on conquest have been able successfully to maintain its independence, is as marvellous as many of the fables of romance. And yet this is in brief the history of Montenegro.‡

* GLADSTONE.

† The population of Montenegro did not reach thirty thousand until the accession of the Berda towards the middle of the last century.

‡ 'In many eyes it must be an ideal land where military service is absolutely universal, where primary instruction is also absolutely universal—I may add, where the ownership of land is universal also. In Montenegro, as in prehistoric

The marvels which run through their history will be better understood after an examination of the physical aspects of the country and a survey of the habits and condition of its people.

Greece, every man goes armed; every man, dressed in the picturesque costume of his tribe, carries his pistol and yataghan in his girdle. But if he can wield pistol and yataghan, he can also turn either to his spade or to his pen. Here, and perhaps here only in the modern world, we can see the very model of a warrior tribe, a nation of a quarter of a million who have known how to maintain their independence with their own right hands, and who at the same time are making rapid strides to a higher place among civilised nations than some of the great powers of the world.'—FREEMAN.

PART I.

COUNTRY AND PEOPLE OF MONTENEGRO.

CHAPTER I.

NAME — BOUNDARIES — SUPERFICIAL EXTENT — PASS FROM CATTARO.

THE reason for one half of the name by which this land of sombre desolate mountains is known in all modern languages has long been matter of dispute. Its cold grey limestone ridges, looking black by contrast with the lighter hue of the Dalmatian hills;* the masses of dark pines, and of other forest trees, which, it is said, once covered large portions of its mountain heights; † the terror with which the

* 'Quiconque aura vu le front calcaire, la face grise des cimes du Monténégro sous les sombres nuées qui les enveloppent en un jour d'orage, comprendra aisément qu'on leur ait donné le nom de Montagne Noire, comme sur les confines du pays de Bade on a donné, à une large et profonde pyramide de sapins le nom de Schwarzwald (Forêt Noire).' — *Lettres sur l'Adriatique et le Monténégro*, par M. X. MARMIER, t. ii. p. 98. See also SIR J. GARDNER WILKINSON's *Dalmatia and Montenegro*, vol. i. p. 402.

† 'All along the road, and in all that I saw of Montenegro, the mountains are of that bluish-grey which darkens so curiously in the afternoons and the winter into rich

Montenegrins inspired the Turkish inhabitants of the lowlands who dwelt along their frontiers; and the name of one of the dynasties which formerly ruled this country *—have been severally assigned by one writer or another as the meaning of part of its name of Monte*negro* in the Venetian dialect of Italian, of *Tzrna*gora in Slavonic, and of *Kara*dagh in Turkish.† Be this as it may, there is no doubt as to the remainder of the name by which the country is known. Politically, as well as geographically and historically, Montenegro is pre-eminently a land of mountains. Its strength, in all wars with Turkey, is due as well to the sterility of the country ‡ as to the inaccessible nature of

purple and absolute black, while in the bright daylight it is only cold grey and at midday almost whitish. But seeing the rock covered with the dark-leaved dwarf oak and other brushwood, which grows out of every crevice in black masses, the traveller recognises at once the meaning of the name so dear to its inhabitants—the Tzerna-Gora, or Black Mountains.'— LADY STRANGFORD'S *Eastern Shores of the Adriatic*, p. 139.

* *Le Monténégro Contemporain*, par G. FRILLEY ET JOVAN WLAHOVITJ. Paris, 1876.

† In pure Italian the name is Montenero, in Greek Mavro Vouni, in Albanian Mal-Esija, and in Arabic maps Aljûbal-al-Aswad, all of which have the same meaning, 'the Black Mountain.'

‡ 'Here a small army is beaten, a large one dies of hunger.'—PATON.

the retreats, from which swarms of irregular soldiers have issued to defend their homes and liberties, and to repel alike the attacks of fanatical hordes and of veteran armies. Its songs, almost its only literature, are inspired by the mountain breeze. The character of its hardy inhabitants is such as is only found in mountainous countries. And the chaos of limestone, either prolonged in short ridges, serrated and rugged with bluff irregular spurs, or bent in a circle enclosing a small plain of fertile land, as the crater is girdled by the sides of a volcano, is the key to the history of this people, and will account in some measure for the success which has crowned their long struggle to maintain their faith and independence, from the day when at Kossova the Serbian power was broken and its monarchy lost, down to our own time, when the troops of Turkey keep ceaseless watch over its northern, eastern, and southern frontiers.* The chronicles of Montenegro are written for the most part in the popular songs which record feats of individual heroism, such as rugged mountain territory alone renders possible, but such as no other highland country can rival.

* 'La nature a été gratuitement elle-même le Vauban des Monténégrins. La nature leur a fait un cercle de remparts, une enceinte continue.'—LENORMANT, *Turcs et Monténégrins*.

Montenegro has the Austrian province of Dalmatia on the south-west, on the other three sides it is bounded by Turkey. The north-eastern frontier of Montenegro, formed by a ridge of the Dinarian Alps, is separated from free Serbia by a strip of broken ground, connecting the provinces of Bosnia and the Herzegovina with the district of Stara Serbia, in the occupation of Turkey. On the north-west it has for its boundary an offset from the same ridge of mountains, running nearly at right angles with the rest of the range, and stretching almost to the Adriatic near Ragusa. Within this line, however, lies the beautiful and fertile vale of Niksic, held by the Turks, although ethnologically, as well as geographically and socially, it is a part of Montenegro, to which indeed it previously belonged. Another mountain ridge, broken by a succession of lofty peaks, of which Mount Vegli Verch and Mount Lovchen* are the highest, shuts out Montenegro from the sea, and forms its south-western boundary. On the south-east towards Albania the frontier differs in character from those on the other three sides. Here the mountain sinks into the plain, the gorges are wider, the breadth of fertile land greater, and the country depends for its defence rather upon

* The Monte Sella of the Italians.

the valour of its sons than upon any feature of nature. At this point the line of separation between Montenegro and Turkey is made up in part of the easy slopes of various mountain ridges, which, however irregular in their formation, have almost always a south-eastern direction; in part by the rivers Zeta and Moratcha and by smaller streams.

Two ideas lie at the root of all Slavonic political organizations, the family and the race, not, as with other people, the individual and the territory. Until 1859 no official limits had been defined between Turkey and this Principality,* and Montenegro meant rather the country occupied by the Montenegrins than a district of country with a rigid line of demarcation, a fact which it is not easy to obliterate from the minds of this people. In 1859, however, a commission appointed by the five chief European powers laid down for the first time with precision the frontier line, which includes the present independent principality of Montenegro. Unhappily for the preservation of peace, this line was drawn with so little regard to the fair claim of this people and to their means of subsistence, that it has added

---

* The boundary between Austria and Montenegro had been settled about thirty years before this date.

a fresh perplexity to the relations between the Porte and the Montenegrins.*

In shape Montenegro has been compared to the leaf of a plane-tree, to which it bears a general resemblance. Perhaps a better idea of its shape may be obtained by joining two right-angled triangles at the apex of each, allowing one somewhat to overlap the other. It lies between 42° 10′ and 42° 56′ of north latitude, and between 18° 41′ and 20° 22′ of east longitude of Greenwich.† The greatest length of the Principality, which is from east to west, is about fifty-five miles; its greatest breadth, from north to south, about thirty-eight miles. In the centre, however, the Turkish territory on both sides indents that of Montenegro so considerably, that its northern frontier—that on the side of Herzegovina—is only distant some twelve miles from the first Turkish post in Albania: an arrangement which seriously impairs the defensive power of the country, and is provocative of fresh struggles between the

---

* 'La délimitation qu'elle résulte du travail de la commission internationale de 1859, ne saurait êtra considérée comme propre à fixer dans l'avenir les limites définitives de la principauté. Ce n'est en effet que par exception que nous y voyons des confins bien naturels et surtout indiscutables, tels que ceux de la Zéta et de la Sitoritza.'—*Le Monténégro Contemporain*, p. 87.

† Or between 16° 1′ and 16° 58′ east longitude of Paris.

Porte and Montenegro. The superficial extent of the Principality is estimated at seventy geographical miles square. The frontier line is, however, so irregular, that the traveller who would trace the line of limitation would have to pass over two hundred and eighty miles before reaching the point from which he started.*

It is not easy to compute the area of Montenegro because of this great irregularity of its frontier; nor, when computed, do the figures give more than an imperfect idea of the quantity of the land that can be brought under cultivation, nor indeed of the real extent of the country, since the sides of the mountains, sterile as they are, are tenanted by peasants who cultivate with the utmost care the smallest patch of ground which has been formed in the hollows and crevices of the mountain slopes by the decay of vegetable matter and by the disintegration of the rocks during long ages. There are few more striking instances of parsimonious industry than that presented to the traveller on his ride from Cattaro to Cetinje—than the small plots, we can scarcely call them fields, of wheat, maize, capsicums, or potatoes lying in the hollows of the rocks. Corn-fields twenty feet by twelve, and

* *Le Monténégro Contemporain*, p. 90.

potato-grounds less than six feet square, are of frequent occurrence.* Such a spectacle of industry can hardly be seen in any other country in the world. In the valleys on the southern frontier, where the country descends on one side towards Lake Skodra,† and on the other overlooks Budua and Antivari on the Adriatic, the soil is not only more fertile than the rest of Montenegro, but agriculture and horticulture have advanced to a degree of perfection which would be observable in any country.‡ There the hills are terrassed for vineyards, and fig and pomegranate orchards add largely to the exports of the Principality.

Most travellers who visit Montenegro enter the

* 'I saw clearings of so small a size as barely to admit of one potato plant or three of maize, and little fields but one yard in diameter.'—*Rambles in Istria, Dalmatia, and Montenegro*, p. 249.

'On a ledge of rock, in a little depression between the rocks, in a niche, in a mere crevice, in short everywhere within possibility, a little field has been made, the stones picked off, the rocks torn out, and, perhaps, earth added artificially; and behold, a patch of potatoes or of maize! Nothing else seems grown here, but I declare that I saw many flourishing little crops not a yard square.'—LADY STRANGFORD's *Eastern Shores of the Adriatic*.

† The Palus Labeatis of LIVY, xliv. 31. Skodra, the Scutari of our maps, is the name of the lake and the city at its southern extremity.

‡ CYPRIEN ROBERT, *Les Slaves de Turquie*, t. i. p. 121.

country from Cattaro in Dalmatia. Immediately above the small city, which is built on the narrow strip of land interposed between the waters of the Bocche and the mountain rampart of the Principality on that side, lies the pass into Montenegro. Viewed from below the road appears drawn along the face of a cliff almost precipitous. It is only, indeed, by a series of zigzags reaching to the top that any road could have been constructed. For about halfway up this road, or ladder (*scala*), as it is properly called, is Austrian, and has been made with all the appliances which military science possesses. This part of the way consists of seventy-three zigzags perfectly well made, smooth, tolerably wide, and guarded at all the angles by a parapet.* For the first three-quarters of an hour the Venetian citadel, which looks very ruinous, hovers above the head of the traveller, and hangs over Cattaro. Passing almost close to this, and by the Morlacco hamlet of Spigliari, the traveller soon quits the territory of Austria and takes leave of the road. From this point the territory of Montenegro begins. The way is left almost in its primitive wildness—a chaos of rocks and water-courses. A pass which no military array could hope to force, and which a handful of such moun-

* LADY STRANGFORD, p. 134.

taineers as Montenegro rears might hold against a large army. The top of this pass, which opens upon the plateau of Niegush, is almost five thousand feet above the level of Cattaro. If the traveller chances to mount this *scala* on a market-day, which apparently is almost every day in the week, he will pass files of mules and small ponies laden with the produce of Montenegro, and groups of men and women, the latter nearly as heavily laden as the animal with bundles of firewood or of sumac, with fruit, vegetables, or flesh, whilst the men, with some exceptions, are unburdened, except with their rifle and long pipe.* In ascending the pass the Montenegrins follow the windings of the road, but in descending these hardy and agile mountaineers usually shorten the distance by leaping from boulder to boulder in a straight descent, where the least false step would lead to almost certain death. After mounting to the top of the pass, if the traveller ascends the adjoining height of the Lovchen, his eye will take in almost

---

* Misses Mackenzie and Irby, speaking of their visit to Cetinje by this *scala*, say expressively, 'Although it was not market-day, the Ladder of Cattaro swarmed with Montenegrins as the ladder of a beehive with bees.'— *Travels in South Slavonic Provinces,* vol. ii. p. 221, second edition. No image brings back to the mind the lively scene better than this.

the whole of Montenegro proper, the plains of Upper Albania with Lake Skodra, together with the long parallel ridges of the Herzegovina and the Berda, and he will thus be able to trace the long lines of mountainous passes which have enabled the people to maintain their independence, or quickly to recover from any momentary reverses of the fortune of war.

The impression which this prospect is calculated to make on a traveller is thus described in a private letter now before me: 'After nearly three hours of toil, partly on foot and partly on horseback, I reached the top of the pass, and was able to look down upon everything within sight. The view was one which will not be soon forgotten. Below me lay the Bocche di Cattaro, smooth as glass, reflecting as clearly as in a mirror the towers and white-fronted houses which rise far above the margin of the sea. Every mountain and ravine, every pathway winding to the top of the ridge opposite to me, every village or town, every vineyard and oliveyard, was sharply defined in the clear atmosphere, and the whole tract of country seemed more like a raised map than solid earth and deep sea. Turning from the road which I had passed over, I was now able to look inland towards Bosnia and Albania, and the sight in this direction, though totally different from that behind me, was not less striking. I seemed to be looking out upon a turbulent sea of grey limestone, an ocean of rolling boulders and petrified breakers.'

CHAPTER II.

RIVERS—MOUNTAINS—GEOLOGY OF MONTENEGRO—
MOUNT LOVCHEN.

THOUGH springs of water gush from the sides of the loftiest mountains, there is, if we except the time when on the melting of the snows they are furrowed for awhile by torrents, a singular absence of anything resembling a cascade in the whole country, and streams which rise here to the dignity of rivers would elsewhere be considered unimportant. Of these the Zeta, or Zenta, which gave its name to the whole country formerly ruled by the Princes of Montenegro, of which the present Principality is but a fragment, rises in the southern declivity of the mountain range to the west of the town of Niksic, and marks for a short distance the boundary between Montenegro and the Herzegovina; it is then lost in the earth, and pursues a subterranean course until it reaches the neighbourhood of Ostrog, when bursting forth again it flows through the beautiful valley of Bielopavolic, and falls into the Moratcha, between Spouj and Podgoritza, near the ruins of Dioclea. The extreme length of this river, including its subterranean course, is about seventeen miles.

The Rjeka, or rather the Tzrnovichi-rjeka,* rises near the little town or village of the same name, and though possessing a larger volume of water than the Zeta, has a shorter course than that river, its length being less than ten miles. It is, however, navigable for large boats or barges almost to its source. It is a characteristic of several of the rivers on the Dalmatian coast of the Adriatic that they burst from their source in a full volume of water. Thus the Rjeka rushes out of a deep arched gloomy cavern, which has been compared to the vast portal of a Gothic cathedral, and after turning the flank of the mountains in which it has its source broadens into a wide sheet of water near the little arsenal of Obod, and having at length hollowed out for itself a deep bed, flows under the arches of a picturesque bridge, and past the village or small town to which it gives its own name, Rjeka. The waters

* This river, because of its importance to Montenegro, is known generally by the name of 'The River' (rjeka).

of this river, after being joined by those of a smaller stream, the Karatuna, near Jablac, fall into the Lake of Skodra. Viewed either from the rocks above or from its surface, this stream is one of rare beauty. Its borders are fringed with the Raketa (*Salix caprea*, Lin.), with pomegranate bushes and fig-trees, and through a great part of the year are gay with the purple blossoms of the former shrub, or afire with the scarlet blossoms of the pomegranate. Except in the character of its vegetation, the Rjeka resembles a highland river, and widens throughout its course into lake-like reaches, which appear to be closed in on all sides by the grey sterile rocks rising from its bed. The effect of this breadth of water is, however, in a great measure, lost, in consequence of the fields of rushes and water-lilies, white and yellow, which cover the whole surface of the water except in the centre of the stream. These form a cover for gulls and other aquatic birds, and shelter numerous families of coots, water-hens, and dab-chicks, or dive-dappers.*
The mouths of the ravines which open upon this river give the traveller glimpses of white-gabled cottages, peeping out of clusters of walnut, cornel, and

---

* 'Dive-dapper,' the old poetic name of the dab-chick.

'Like a dive-dapper peering through a wave.'
SHAKSPERE, *Venus and Adonis*.

pomegranate trees. A third river, the Tzrnitza, has its source in the mountains of Triroga, overhanging the Bay of Spizza, near the junction of the Turkish, Austrian, and Montenegrin frontiers. This river is the shortest of any of the streams which rise in Montenegro. It falls, like all the others, into the Lake of Skodra, at the north-western corner. It is navigable for boats only for a short distance above Vir-bazar at its mouth. The Moratcha, the most considerable of these rivers, though it rises within Montenegro, near the foot of Mount Dormitor, on the north-eastern angle of the Principality, flows through the Berda in a general south-western direction, loses the character of a Montenegrin river for a great part of its course, and runs exclusively through the Turkish territory of Albania, where, augmented by the waters of the Zeta, it passes the town of Podgoritza, and falls into the Lake of Skodra. This river is navigable from its mouth up to Podgoritza, but ceases to be so where it runs through Montenegrin territory. In addition to these rivers there are also some small rivulets, which acquire importance in the general deficiency of water in large districts of this country.* The Mala rjeka, the Brestica,

---

* The Ribnitza (*fish-river*) rises at the foot of the mountains on the frontier of the Koutchi nahia, and falls into the

the Matica, and Sitanica, which fall into the Moratcha—these, though full of water in the winter and spring, are almost dry, and hardly to be traced, in the summer and autumn months. The peculiar surface, combined with the absorbent nature of the limestone rocks, prevents the accumulation of water into rivulets and streams. Even wells are extremely rare. The inhabitants are therefore obliged to collect rain-water in cisterns for their household use and for their cattle.*

The principality of Montenegro is divided into Montenegro proper, on the west, and the Berda, on the east. The former is for the most part a rocky, irregular plateau, rising on the north upwards of four thousand feet above the level of the sea, but falling in a rapid descent towards the south,† basin-shaped depressions like enormous craters; and valleys or gorges resembling deep chasms occur throughout the broken table-land; whilst from the rocky plateau itself solitary peaks and short irregular ridges of mountains rise to a great height above the rough

Moratcha near Podgoritza. It belongs, however, to Albania rather than to Montenegro.

* Paper of COUNT KARACZAY on Albania in *Journal of Royal Geographical Society*, vol. xii. p. 48.

† 'Entre Cettigne et le lac de Scutari, la différence de niveau est d'environ 1,200 mètres pour une distance de 24 kilometres.'—DELARUE, *Le Monténégro*, p. 19.

base from which they spring, looking at a distance like the waves of a storm-tossed sea suddenly turned into stone.* This great plateau, Montenegro proper, terminates eastward at the valley of Bielopavolic and the banks of the Zeta. The Berda,† though a great part of it is, like the western part of the Principality, an irregular plain of mountain country rather than a land of mountain ranges, is here and there broken by a succession of wild irregular valleys, and partakes more than Western Montenegro of the general character of mountainous countries, a land of steep precipitous ridges rising directly from the plain. Though these peaks and broken ridges lie for the most part in the interior of the country and on the northern or Herzegovinian frontier, yet Vegli Verch, a little to the north of Risano, rises considerably above the average height of the rest of the mountains; whilst Mount Lovchen, which towers above Cattaro, is one of the three most considerable of the mountain heights of the Tzrnagora.

---

* 'Suivant une légende, Dieu, lorsqu'il créa le monde, disposant les vallées et les Montagnes, portait dans un sac les pierres nécessaires à son œuvre. Le sac, usé par un long service, se déchira et les rochers tombant formerent ce chaos de pierres nommé plus tard Monténégro.'—DELARUE.

† 'Berda,' plural of 'berdo,' a mountain.

Mount Korm, or Kom,* on the south-east angle of Montenegro, which projects like a bastion into the frontier of Albania, rises in two peaks to an estimated height of from seven thousand five hundred to eight thousand feet above the level of the sea, and is covered with snow during greater part of the year. The other mountains attain an elevation at the most of five thousand feet. Mount Dormitor, on the north-east angle of Montenegro, and overlooking Bosnia and the Herzegovina, is estimated to be of equal height to Mount Korm.† Montenegro, however, it must be borne in mind, is not so much a mountainous country as a mountain mass, hollowed by fissures and penetrated by occasional gorges, which open occasionally into valleys of moderate width.

The valleys throughout the Principality are seldom more than three or four miles long, nor wider than one mile. The valley of the Zeta, however, is an

---

* *Kom*, the Arabic 'mountain,' the *cumulus* of the Latins, is the name given to some mountains in Turkey, generally such as are isolated. This is the name given to a mountain islet in the Lake Skodra, near the Montenegrin frontier.

† 'La hauteur de ces trois montagnes est à peu pres la même, et peut s'evaluer à 2,500 mètres au-desous du niveau de la mer. Dans l'interieur du pays aucun sommet n'atteint cette altitude, et les crêtes sont escarpées plutot qu'élévées."—LENORMANT, *Turcs et Monténégrins*.

exception to this. It is in some parts nearly six miles wide, and is cultivated to a distance of nearly three miles on each side of the river.* In this valley occur almost the only hedgerows found in Montenegro.

The geological formation of the Principality is for the most part compact grey limestone, passing in some places into marble, with occasional instances of dolomite. The plains in the south are of the same character as those of North Albania, which they join: a coarse conglomerate, so coarse, indeed, as to be scarcely distinguished from the ruins of Roman masonry, which abound in all directions on the frontier of Montenegro. On the opposite side of the country, overlooking the vale of Niksic, the traveller will meet with singular deposits of small pebbles thrown up in heaps as on a sea-beach, and almost as difficult to walk over as the loose stones of a sea-shore. Lignite is found near the banks of the Rjeka; and it has been satisfactorily ascertained that there are, in the province of Tzrnitza, near Lake Skodra, deposits of anthracite coal of considerable extent, though, so far as experiments have tested its qualities, apparently but of small value. Of the value, however, of such coal it is impossible to speak

* *Journal of Geographical Society*, vol. xii. (1842), p. 51.

with any certainty, since the geology of Montenegro has never been investigated.* Probably, when the country has been carefully explored by scientific travellers, the limestone ridges will be found of greater importance than they seem at present. As yet the chief value of these ridges is in the supply of stone for the purpose of building. The hardness of this stone and the polish which it takes render it well adapted for this; and it supplies the only material of which palace and churches, monasteries and peasants' cabins, alike are built.

As one of the great objects of attraction in Montenegro is the summit of the Lovchen mountain, and as I have not seen it elsewhere described, I extract from my note-book the account of a day spent there a few years since. To the lover of the picturesque the view from the top is the finest, as it is also the most extensive, in the whole Principality. To the Montenegrin it has another charm; it is the burial-place of the late Vladika, Peter the Second,

* Dr. Barth, the celebrated African traveller, contemplated making a careful geological survey of Montenegro. This project, however, was frustrated by his early death. The best geological survey of Montenegro, so far as I know, is the *Aperçu Géologique de Monténégro*, by COLONEL KOVALEVOKY, in the *Annales de la Géologie*. Paris, 1842-43.

great-uncle to the reigning Prince, and the last bishop who united in his person the civil and ecclesiastical power over Montenegro. Having arranged over night to visit this shrine, I rose at five o'clock in the morning, and by half-past five was in the saddle and on my way to the Lovchen, accompanied by M. Vaclic, the secretary of the Prince, and Captain Zegar, of the Austrian army. For the first half-hour of the journey our way lay across the sandy plain of Cetinje; at the end of that time we began to mount by a road which was a perfect chaos of stones, along which I left it to my horse to pick his way as he chose, satisfied that my reason was not equal to his sagacity in this matter. A road certainly there was, but one on which no constructive skill had ever been exerted. When I looked at it, the thought flashed across my mind that the couplet of the Irish road-overseer in the Highlands was after all very sensible. The appropriateness of the words was so great that I could not drive the jingle out of my head:—

> "If you'd seen these roads before they were made,
> You'd have held up your hands and have bless'd General Wade."

Here certainly were the roads, but as yet wholly unmade; so that another generation of Montenegrins may have reason, like their brother mountaineers, to bless some future road-maker who will do for them what the luckless Hanoverian general did for the Highlands of Scotland.

After about three hours' scramble over the boulders which were strewed along our path, past hazel hedges and through beech scrub and fern brake, up precipitous heights, along dangerously narrow ridges of rock, and down into sunless ravines, we at length reached the foot of the mountain which we were to climb. Our path now was across a limestone ledge, which at a distance looked as though it had been turned up by some gigantic plough, probably in the prehistoric age. A precipitous descent on one side and a sharp slope on the other, without vegetation of any kind, compelled us to be cautious. At length we dismounted at the base of the lofty height in which the mountain terminates. Rude stairs, partly worn by the course of time, and in part cut for this purpose, lead to the top of the ascent on which stands the small mortuary chapel which is the object of so many pilgrimages by the people of Montenegro, as well as by strangers. This chapel was built by the Vladika, Peter II., and contains the tomb in which he left directions that he should be buried. When his death took place, his nephew and successor Danilo was absent in Vienna; and on his return he found, to his regret, that the difficulty of the ascent, and probably the wish that the body of their revered chief should rest in the midst of the people over whom he had ruled with so much advantage to them, had led the Montenegrins to disregard his wishes, and to inter his body at Cetinje. As a law inexorable as that of the Medes and Persians prohibits the removal or the disturbing in any way of a body until it has been buried five years, Prince Danilo was unable to carry out the wishes of the Vladika for that length of time. When, however, the five years had expired, the body was removed from Cetinje to its present resting-place at the top of Mount Lovchen. The chapel is a very simple one, and, though built only in 1845, is, from defects in its construction, already partially in ruins. It consists of a vaulted dome surmounting a round chapel of some twelve feet diameter, with a small recess or sanctuary at the east end. In this is a small altar. There is neither iconostasis nor furniture of any kind. The tomb occupies the whole south side of the chapel, and from its size recalls the memory of the gigantic stature of the Vladika who lies buried within. The part of the mountain on which it stands seems intended as the base for some such building as this, for after rising gradually and at a moderate angle, the top of the Lovchen consists of a small rugged plateau resting on a precipitous base above the rest, and apparently placed on it, rather than itself forming a part of the mountain. In fact it resembles a gigantic pedestal. This is the part which we found it necessary to ascend on our feet. This pedestaled top is entirely destitute of vegetation, except that some few tufts of long coarse grass, and a wild thorn or two springing from the fissures of the rock, are found there.

But however difficult and fatiguing the ascent to the top of the mountain, and however sterile the summit, all is forgotten in the singular but magnificent view which bursts upon the sight of the traveller as he stands beside the chapel-tomb. The eye then roams over the tops of the mountains of Montenegro, without seeing the plains which lie between their ridges, or getting a glimpse of the crater-like hollows which are to be found on almost all the heights. Grey in its silent sterility, the spectator seems to be looking down upon a stony sea, in which, without hyperbole, the waves may be said to be running mountains high. The woods of stunted oak and beech, which clothe with a scanty robe the sides of the mountains, are lost to the sight; and the few traces of vegetation which may be seen appear like floating seaweed on the surface of the ocean. On one side the view embraces, as in a panorama, the whole of Montenegro, several ranges of mountains in Bosnia, great part of the Herzegovina, the large Lake of Skodra in Albania, and the adjacent plain veined with the silvery streams of water which fall into the lake. On another side is the Bocche di Cattaro, with every feature of the varied shore sharply defined; and beyond this the dark Adriatic, on the bosom of which can be seen the snowy sails of its merchant vessels and the smoke of the passing steamboats.

This is the general aspect of the scene. By going, however, to the edge of the precipice and looking down upon the country immediately below, the traveller gets a totally different view. He then sees not only solitary homesteads, but groups of cottages and fertile fields, and the vale between the opposite mountains, the limestone ridge on the top of which he is standing, seems alive with flocks of sheep and goats, and with men and women busied with the tillage of their fields.*

* Mariano Bolezza appears to have enjoyed the same view, and found things in 1614 much the same as a traveller may

And now, when we had examined this singular scene, our attendants, whose number, by accessions from the farm cottages which we had visited, had swelled to eight, brought us a pail of new milk, and a large lump of frozen snow from some caverns at the foot of the Lovchen. This, with the aid of provisions brought with us from Cetinje, some bottles of good Montenegrin wine, ham, cold chicken, and excellent cheese, supplied us with a meal, for which the long journey and the clear mountain air had duly prepared us. Then came the invariable mid-day slumber, or at least rest, our attendants skilfully availing themselves of projecting pieces of the rock, and thus finding shelter from the blaze of the noonday sun. At three o'clock we scrambled down to the point where we had left our horses, and, sometimes on horseback and sometimes on foot, as the nature of the ground compelled, we reached the base of the mountain—it would be a misnomer to say that we reached the plain, as the

---

find them at the present day. He speaks with delight of the view from the summit: 'Quando è sereno,' embracing 'verso levante Durazzo et Scuttari;' whilst at its base he notes the Peccorella, 'Si che pasciutasi et abeverata se ne riposa le più arse hore del giorno, sotto à grandissimi, numerosissimi et amenissimi faggi, alberi, frasini, zappini che le fan'ombra tutto il giorno.'—*Relazione*.

low ground was nearly as rough as we had found the sides of the mountain in the course of our descent.

On reaching the bottom of the Lovchen we were invited to rest at the house of one of our attendants, and to eat roasted eggs and more ham, which for compliment's sake we did. This enabled me for the first time to see an ordinary Montenegrin cottage. It consisted of one room built with stone without cement, the floor being the bare earth. When I entered cooking was going on, and for a time the smoke, which escaped on all sides, prevented me from seeing anything. When I was accustomed to this I found two little children, half naked, crawling on the floor and trying to get away from the stranger. Children generally in Montenegro dread strangers. Besides these two children, my host had the care of two belonging to a brother killed in the recent war with the Turks, and also the mother of these children, so that there was no room to spare in the cottage; but then in this climate there is for the greater part of the year the 'out-of-doors,' which is of unlimited dimensions. The little patches of corn, potatoes, and other vegetables in front of this cottage were, like similar pieces of ground throughout Montenegro, very clean; indeed, not a weed was to be seen. What the people of

Serbia have no notion of—namely, the value of manure and the necessity of keeping the ground free from weeds—their Montenegrin brothers generally seem to understand thoroughly. Their little fields are usually fenced in with walls of uncemented stones as this one was. Behind the house was a good-sized pigsty, and farther away were several beehives. The little niece of my host was watching a goat and a few sheep, and preventing them from wandering into the potato-garden and from getting among the maize; and the bowl of milk which was placed before me indicated the possession of cows, though I saw no signs of them. After resting and doing justice to the hospitality of our attendant, who was one of the Prince's guards, we again mounted, and reached Cetinje about seven o'clock in the evening.

CHAPTER III.

CLIMATE—PRODUCTION—EXPORTS AND IMPORTS—ROADS.

THE soil of most part of Montenegro is of so porous a character that after a few hours no trace remains of the heaviest rains, and the hay-crops are often burnt up during the prolonged drought of summer. Some small streams, after a short course, are altogether absorbed, and disappear underground.* The plain around Cetinje, the capital, girdled by high crags, and resembling the huge crater of an extinct volcano, is almost wholly composed of sand, as though it had once been the bed of the sea. Were it not that the excessive dryness of the climate is in part corrected by the dense fogs of the Adriatic, which

* 'Quelquesunes rentrent tout à coup dans les entrailles du sol, comme si elles s'ennuyaient de leur voyage dans notre monde trop truyant, comme si la nostalgie les ramenait sous le dôme de leur silencieux empire.'—MARMIER.

bring with them torrents of rain, this territory would be utterly sterile, and the few rivers which flow through it would be soon dried up. Delarue thus describes one of these fogs and its attendant fall of rain:—*

'Some days after my arrival in Montenegro I witnessed one of those storms which are so welcome during the intense heat of summer. About seven o'clock in the evening a dense fog covered the whole plain. The darkness was so great that the nearest objects were invisible. The rain fell in sheets of water; the lightnings played along the heights which rise around the basin of Cetinje, and crowned them with circles of fire. All night long and until the next day the thunder crashed without intermission. When morning came the plain around the capital wore the appearance of a swamp, and broad pools covered the whole of the ground. The corn was entirely under water, and the wells, which the evening before were almost dry, were now overflowing. Every trace of the storm, every vestige of water, disappeared during the day.'

The dry clear climate of the high grounds enables the Montenegrin to be heard, and even to carry on conversation, at a great distance. From ridge to

* *Le Monténégro*, par HENRI DELARUE.

ridge, to an incredible distance, they are able to communicate any news of importance, or to summon the armed array and direct its movements, without the need of signals for the eye. To use the words of a French traveller, they are thus able to dispense with the help of the electric telegraph, and each one becomes for himself a living telegraph (*S'eriger eux mêmes en télégraphes vivants*).* This power of making themselves heard, and the practice of talking at a great distance, is thought to give a loudness and sharpness of tone to their customary voice. 'To be heard continuously, so as to be heard for miles off, is a highly valued accomplishment.' †

The different elevation of the various districts of Montenegro causes some diversity of climate. In the south, where the country is more depressed, the summers are scorching and the winters mild. In the north, where the country is much higher than on the Albanian frontier, the breezes which sweep across Hungary temper the heat of summer though they increase the rigour of winter. Here there is much cold weather in the autumn and spring. On the highlands snow remains for most part of the

---

* MARMIER, t. ii. p. 112.
† *Travels in Slavonic Provinces of Turkey*, vol. ii. p. 223.

year, and Rjeka is smiling with the luxuriant verdure of June whilst the heights overlooking the town are white with the snows of December.

This difference of climate according to the different elevations of the stony plateau gives variety to the productions of Montenegro. In the north, wheat, rye and barley, maize, capsicums, and a little tobacco are reared. In the south, vines, pomegranates, figs, peaches, apples, cherries, citrons, oranges, olives, mulberries, and tobacco are the chief productions. Cabbages, cauliflowers, potatoes, white and scarlet runners, pease, melons, radishes, and onions grow around almost every cottage, and supply food alike for the peasant and his family as well as for the litter of pigs in the sty, which yield them the chief part of their animal food. In the swamps near the source of the Rjeka, Mirko, the father of the reigning Prince, had a few years since several fields of rice, and on the hills between Danilograd and Selo-Gradatz, the same warrior farmer had an experimental plantation of coffee; what success, however, he met with in his attempts to increase the number of the productions of Montenegro, I am unable to say. The potato was introduced into the country in 1786 by the Vladika Peter I., and the cultivation of the root extended in a very short time throughout the whole Principality, where it is largely used by the inhabitants. It is also sold by them in considerable quantities in the adjacent market towns of Turkey and Austria.

According to Sir Gardner Wilkinson, the common trees of this country, in addition to those just enumerated, are the oak, ilex, beech, ash, acacia, firs, hazels, wild pears, poplars, larches, cypresses, pines, yews, chestnuts, planes, limes, willows, and alders. The underwood on the hillsides consists of oak and beech scrub, arbutus, juniper, rosemary, myrtle, blackberry, and other brambles, and where the ground is not covered with these shrubs, savoury wild thyme and mint scent the air, and a profusion of clematis and other wild flowers climb the rocks on all sides, and furnish the pasture-ground from which the excellent honey of Montenegro is extracted.* These wild flowers, I believe, are the only flowers in Montenegro, except in the nahia of Tzrnitza. Ground is too precious to be used for unproductive purposes; and ornamental flowers are, so far as my experience serves, unknown. Perhaps the most valuable of all the trees in Montenegro is the scottano, or Venus sumach (*Rhus cotinus*), which grows

* *Voyage Historique et Politique au Monténégro*, par COL. VIALLA DE SOMMIÈRES, t. i. p. 175.

in considerable quantities in the Katunska nahia; the wood and leaves of this tree are much esteemed for tanning and dyeing, and large quantities are exported to Trieste, to Ancona, and to Marseilles.* The mulberry-tree, chiefly the white variety, is cultivated by most of the cottagers in the southern part of the country; and silk is fast becoming one of the most important articles which are exported from Montenegro. Around Danilograd are nursery-grounds belonging to the Prince, and in these large quantities of mulberry-trees are reared and distributed gratuitously to any peasant who may desire them. In the war of 1862 the army of Omar Pasha, however, penetrated as far as this village, and destroyed every tree which Prince Danilo had planted. The same war against this tree was pursued wherever the Turkish soldiers reached; and though the mulberry plantation at Danilograd again flourishes, the trees are but young, and it will take many years to repair the waste made by the troops of Turkey.

Sheep and goats are reared in great numbers throughout Montenegro, especially on the mountain slopes and in the valleys of the Berda. Their flesh, fresh or salted, supplies the markets on the frontier,

---

* The sumac of Montenegro is considered superior to that of Sicily for the purpose of dyeing.

and their skins and wool are largely exported. The smoke-dried mutton (*castradina*) of these mountains is well known in the markets of Istria and Venice, and is purchased in large quantities for the supply of the Austrian navy. Other productions which are exported are dried fish (*scoranza*), tortoise-shell, wax, honey, hides, figs, olives, butter, cheese, tallow, dyewood, firewood, charcoal, cattle, sheep, pigs, mats, ice, maize, vegetables, silk, and tobacco.* A large proportion of these productions is carried across the Turkish and Austrian frontiers and shipped to distant countries. The potatoes, onions, and other vegetables of Montenegro, supply the markets of Cattaro and Podgoritza, whilst the wine of Tzrnitza has acquired a reputation for its sound and wholesome qualities. An inconsiderable quantity of this wine, however, passes the frontiers of the Principality. All these various productions would probably be reared in greater quantities for exportation if there were any prospect of a market and remunerative prices. The heavy transit dues of Austria, however, deprive the labourers of much of their fair profits. It is one of the hardships which press upon

---

* The districts of Liechanska, of Tzrnitza, and Bielopavlic produce good tobacco, which brings a good price in the neighbouring markets of Turkey and Austria.

this people, that they are debarred from the small and, to Turkey, almost useless ports at the foot of the mountains, such as Spizza and Antivari. Were they in the possession of Montenegro, these outlets for their produce and their energies would have prevented many a war with Turkey. In justice to this latter power, it must be recorded that the Porte, it is generally believed, would long since have yielded them to the Montenegrins but for the interference of Austria, fearful lest the existence of a free port so near her Dalmatian territory would interfere with the monopoly which her goods possess, and give to English fabrics an entrance into the markets of the northern and western provinces of European Turkey.

A recent writer enumerates the chief articles of exportation, and thus gives, with some corrections, the following estimate of their value:*—

Meat, salted or smoked . .	£25,000
Cattle	85,000
Pigs	20,000
Fish, fresh or salted . . .	6,500
Silk, cocoons, and silkworm eggs	5,000
Carried forward	£141,500

* *Le Monténégro Contemporain*, p. 115.

Brought forward	£141,500
Shumac	1,500
Pellitory (*Pyréthre insecticide*) .	3,000
Cheese, butter, eggs, fruit .	2,600
Wool	1,000
Firewood	2,000
	£151,600

Wine, brandy, wheat, maize, and tobacco are not enumerated, since these articles are only exported in small quantities. The chief articles of importation are furniture and agricultural implements, cloth, linen, coffee, salt, lead, powder, and firearms.* In 1867 Turkey conceded to the Montenegrins the right to import without duty two millions of okes (upwards of two thousand tons) of salt, by way of the Bojano and Skodra. Afterwards this amount was diminished one-half; but at the time when the present war broke out Montenegro possessed the right of importing about eleven hundred tons of salt

* 'Comme leur besoins sont fort peu considérables, la somme des exportations surpasse notablement celle des importations. Ainsi pour l'année 1860, la dernière dont nous possédions les chiffres officiels, l'ensemble du commerce extérieur des Monténégrins est monté à un total de 1,305,000 francs, dont 992,000 francs pour les sorties et 313,000 francs seulement pour les entrées.'—LENORMANT.

free of duty to Turkey. Most of this is used in salting flesh and fish, afterwards exported. All other articles are subject to heavy import dues paid to that power or to Austria. The moneys which circulate in Montenegro are chiefly Austrian ducats, zwanzigs, and kreutzers. The Montenegrins, however, are well acquainted with the value of English, French, Turkish, and Russian coins.

The *scoranza* (*ouklieva*, Serb, the *Mugil cephalus* of Linnæus), which is an important item in the exports from Montenegro, leaves the Lake of Skodra in the month of September, and finds its way into the Rjeka, where it is taken in great quantities, cured, and exported to Turkey, Dalmatia, and Italy. In size and flavour these fish resemble sardines, and they are excellent whether salted or fresh.* This fishery is the property of the Government, and is of such importance to the Montenegrins that the season for taking the fish is formally opened by a state visit of the Prince, who comes for this purpose with his court to Plush, a village situated on a rock jutting out from the right bank of the Rjeka.

Though the scoranza is the chief article of commerce, the rivers throughout Montenegro abound in other kinds of fish. The trout, which is excellent

* WILKINSON, vol. i. p. 415.

in flavour, attains to an enormous size. Sir Gardner Wilkinson mentions some white trout which weighed twenty okes, or sixty pounds,* and there are traditions of fish larger even than these. The trout in these rivers are of two kinds—the white, which attains a large size, and a smaller kind, salmon in the colour of its flesh, and more delicate as food. The eels of the Rjeka are also large and excellent in quality, as well as considerable in size, and in addition perch and carp are taken in great numbers. Martino Bolizza, a native of Cattaro, in the beginning of the seventeenth century (1614), celebrated the abundance and excellency of the fish in the rivers of Montenegro, and they have not degenerated in these respects since his time.

Game is not abundant, though hares and rabbits are found; the bird most in request is the red-legged partridge. Wild ducks, however, frequent Lake Skodra; the traveller may see flocks of wild pigeons in many parts of the country, and the black-cock is not an uncommon bird. Those who prefer the more exciting objects of the chase may, in addition to the stag, the roebuck, and fallow deer, chance to meet with the bear, especially on the Bosnian frontier, the fox, the lynx, and the wolf, which in

* WILKINSON, vol. i. p. 532.

sharp winters prowls even to the neighbourhood of Cetinje, and the wild boar, which makes its lair on the banks of the Moratcha. As to the smaller birds, the absence of forest-land in one-half of the Principality, and the infrequency of hedgerows everywhere, may, perhaps, account for so few song-birds visiting Montenegro. Flocks of starlings, however, Royston crows, and magpies may be seen on the open ground, and coots, water-hens, and gulls are common on the rivers; whilst hawks, eagles, and occasionally a vulture, hold undisputed possession of the mountain solitudes. The rocks, which abound in fissures, shelter large numbers of lizards of various kinds. Travellers are also cautioned against the viper, the bite of which is frequently fatal. In that part of the country which is near Lake Skodra tortoises swarm, and attain a size which makes their shells valuable as an article of commerce.

The extent and state of the public roads are sometimes assumed as criterions by which to test the social condition of a nation. This, however, would not afford a true test of Montenegrin civilisation. Here a bad road has hitherto been a cherished political institution. Surrounded on all sides by watchful enemies, in an almost chronic state of warfare with Turkey, coveted by Austria, and more than desired by the first Napoleon, the maintenance of Montenegrin independence has been a hindrance to the construction of such roads as the commerce of the country, and even the necessities of the simple social life of its inhabitants, would seem to demand. In the time of the Vladika Peter I., the Emperor Napoleon offered in vain to construct a road from Cattaro to Cetinje, probaby with a view of extending it to Skodra. However inconvenient to the traveller the want of good roads may be, what is of far greater consequence, the safety of the country, is best maintained without them; and this consideration in past times prevented their construction, except to a very limited extent. The present Prince, however, has, like his predecessor, Prince Danilo, constructed several roads for interior communication. Long use and highland agility render the rough road of the Principality as easy to its inhabitants as level ground. Between Cetinje and Rjeka the Vladika Peter II. constructed what on the whole must be considered a fair road; and between most villages paths have been formed which diminish the fatigue of travelling without impairing the defensible nature of the country. The road from Rjeka, running south along the precipitous heights overlooking the left bank of the river of the same name, is of this description:

wide enough at the narrowest point for two horsemen to pass—at least with some manœuvring—easy for the sure-footed and agile horses of the country, but capable of being blocked and destroyed in the face of any hostile force which might attempt to penetrate into Montenegro from the Albanian frontier.

The state of the roads throughout the country being such as I have described, it is scarcely necessary to remark that carts and carriages are unknown in any part of Montenegro, and that horses are rare. Except in the district of Tzrnitza, probably four wheels are not to be found in the whole of the mountain territory, and few persons mount on horseback except the chief and the Perianik guards.

CHAPTER IV.

POLITICAL DIVISIONS—CETINJE—NIEGUSH—RJEKA—DIOCLEA—OSTROG.

THE principality of Montenegro is divided into two provinces, Montenegro proper and the Berda. The former lies to the west, and is bounded chiefly by the dominions of the Emperor of Austria; the latter, lying to the east, reaches almost to the frontiers of Serbia, and is wholly bounded by Albania and Bosnia. The valley of Bielopavlic,* through which the river Zeta flows, separates these two portions of the territory of the Prince of Montenegro. Montenegro proper is divided into four *nahias* or provinces:†
Katunska, Tzrnitza, Rjetska, and Liechanska.

Of these four provinces the first is of the chief

---

* The district of Bielopavlic is so called from a certain Bielo-Paulo,' or Paul the White (white probably in the sense of handsome), who took refuge here soon after the battle of Kossova in 1389, and whose descendants still possess much of the land of this nahia.—UBICINI.

† *Nahia,* an Arabic word adopted by the Turks for a

political importance, from its vicinity to Cattaro, its extent, and from its containing Cetinje, the capital of the United Principality, and Niegush, the hereditary home of the reigning family. This province has also fair claims to be regarded as the innermost citadel of Montenegrin independence. Its almost inaccessible gorges and sterile heights have furnished in past times a secure refuge when Turkish armies have overrun the rest of the country, and have even penetrated to Cetinje. Descending from the crags, which none but a veteran highlander could climb, the patriot bands of Montenegro have more than once compelled the Turkish commanders to withdraw from the plain around Cetinje, to abandon their hardly-won vantage ground, and to retreat with heavy loss into Albania.

But though politically the province of Katunska is the most important of all those into which the Principality is divided, economically it is—considering its size—of but small value. No river fertilises the fields of this nahia, and as a consequence it contains, in proportion to its extent, less soil capable of cultivation than any other of the provinces into

canton or district, literally "a portion," or, as a French writer translates the word, "a department." *Plemena*, in the singular *pleme*, is a Serb name for an agglomeration of families of the same origin.

which Montenegro is divided. The traveller to this country, whose route almost always lies across the nahia of Katunska, naturally forms a less favourable idea of the agricultural capabilities of the Principality than if he were to approach Cetinje by the valley of the Rjeka, or by crossing the mountains from Antivari. In this latter case his course would lie through the Tzrnitza, and though the grandeur of the scenery would remind him that he was still in Montenegro, the quantity of land under cultivation, the white-gabled cottages, each peeping out of its separate croft and surrounded by an apple-garden fenced in by pomegranate and fig-trees and ringing with the joyous shouts of children, the bleating of sheep and goats, and the audible murmur of bees, would impress him far differently than the long sterile solitude which he had traversed under a scorching sun from the top of the pass over Cattaro until he reached the sandy waste which lies around Cetinje, a solitude only broken by the village of Niegush, but with scarcely a patch of fertile soil, and, except at one point, destitute of trees. But though the road from the Austrian frontier to the Montenegrin capital is stern, and the scanty soil gives austerity to the view, the valleys which lie off the road and under the shadow of the

Lovchen mountain are fertile by nature, are productive by industry, and remind the traveller of some of the fairest parts of Switzerland, whilst they support as numerous and hardy a race of small peasant proprietors as are to be met with in that country. At the last census the province of Katunska contained nearly 64,000 inhabitants, almost a fourth of the whole population of Montenegro and the Berda. This nahia is subdivided into thirteen plemena (communes or tribes), each pleme being again divided into cela. There are one hundred and fifty-two of these cela in the whole thirteen plemena of the Katunska nahia. The other nahias are subdivided in the same way into plemena, and these further divided into cela. Thus the Tzrnitza nahia has seven plemena and seventeen cela; Rjetska five, with thirty cela; and Liechanska three, with fourteen cela; or in all twenty-eight communes in Montenegro proper, and two hundred and thirteen cela.*

The Tzrnitza nahia possesses the richest soil of all the districts of Montenegro, and its neighbourhood to the Lake of Skodra, which forms part of

---

* The numbers of the plemena vary in accounts of travellers, chiefly from the circumstance that Grahova and Joupan, the two districts added to Montenegro in 1858, are sometimes rendered apart; officially, however, they are portions of the Katunska nahia.

its eastern boundary, together with its proximity to Budua and Antivari, give it a commercial importance which is not possessed by any other nahia. The poorest district as well as the smallest, the least defensible by natural advantages, and consequently the nahia most exposed to the hostile attacks of the Turks, is that of Liechanska, which extends from the Turkish fortress of Spouj to the neighbourhood of Jablac. Like Montenegro proper, the Berda is divided into four nahias: those of Bielopavlic, being further subdivided into three communes, Peperi into three, Moratska into three, and Vasojevichi into five, to which may now be added the Koutchi. This last, having joined Montenegro in 1835-6, took umbrage at the imposition of taxes in 1843, and separated in that year from Montenegro, returning, however, to its former allegiance at the commencement of the present war between Montenegro and the Porte.*

The last-named nahia is Roman Catholic; the other parts of Montenegro belong to the Orthodox

* 'The Koutska nahia was originally independent of Montenegro, but, about 1835-36, the people put themselves under the authority of the Vladika, sent a senator to Tzetinie, and enjoyed the privileges of the other departments, until, taking umbrage at the imposition of taxes, they seceded in 1843 from their allegiance.' This nahia returned to their allegiance to the Prince of Montenegro at the beginning of the present war, and the refusal to give these people up to

Church, and acknowledge the authority of the Metropolitan, who has his seat at Cetinje. The nahias of the Berda are sometimes spoken of as the First, Second, Third, and Fourth Berda, and comprise twenty-five plemena. The nahias of the Berda contain eighteen communes, or aggregation of families, and one hundred and thirty-six cela. Each *nahia* is governed by a sirdar and a voivode, their civil and military commanders. In like manner each *pleme,* or commune, has two chiefs, a kniez and a berakdar, or flag-bearer. Each *pleme* is again divided into *cela* (sing. *celo*), sometimes translated villages, but meaning really village territories. Each of these cela has a judge or head man elected by the members of the celo.* Thus the pleme of Cetinje has seven cela, Niegush ten.† Each *celo* is further divided into *koutcha,* or houses, tenanted

---

the Porte was one of the two points which led to the negociations for peace between Turkey and Montenegro being broken off.

* 'Le Tsernogore ne referme ni villes in forteresses, à peine a-t-il des villages, car ce qu'on appelle de ce nom au Tsernogore n'est que le terrain souvent très-variable occupé par une confrério (*bratstvo*), c'est-à-dire la réunion des différents ménages composent une communauté dont tous les membres se regardent comme parents.'— CYPRIEN ROBERT, t. i. p. 118.

† See for all these details the *Czrna Gora Beljeshke* of the Archimandrite Douchich. Belgrade, 1874.

by a family owning one head. These undivided families may consist, however, of several generations.

Between those who say that, with some three or four exceptions, Montenegro possesses no villages, and those who reckon the number of the villages scattered throughout the country at some six or seven hundred, the difference is rather verbal than real. In the English use of the word there are very few villages, and no town, with the single exception of Rjeka. When the capital of the country, the seat of Government and the residence of the Prince and Archbishop, consists of about sixty houses, it is not to be expected that the villages will be populous. Except Niegush and Rjeka, most villages are too inconsiderable to deserve that name.* In no other country, at least in Europe, would three or four cottages, detached, but standing at a greater or less distance from each other, be called a village. In fact, the *celo*, or village, of Montenegro is a territorial division of the *pleme*, or tribe, and the *celo* is made up of scattered houses, *koutcha*—that is, of families, more or less numerous, aggregated together. When, then, we read, according to a recent census, of 11,811

---

* 'The largest does not contain a population of 1,200 souls.'—WILKINSON, vol. i. p. 406. Delarue estimates that an average village should consist of thirty or forty houses, and contain about 170 inhabitants (*Le Monténégro*, p. 27).

houses in the Principality,* we must remember that this does not mean cottages divided by a party-wall, but families owning obedience to one head, and preserving a family relationship,† and numbering, in some cases, as many as sixty or seventy men able to bear arms.‡ The small farmsteads and cottages throughout this country, whether standing alone or clustered near each other in villages, are built with reference to convenience in the culture of the land, rather than to safety, in accessible not inaccessible sites, principally in hollows and on the slopes of the mountains, none on the points of hills, as in the neighbouring provinces of Turkey.§ This is in keeping with the self-dependent, fearless character of these mountaineers. The same fearlessness has led the Montenegrin peasants to build their cottages detached instead of seeking to cluster them together. This custom, coupled with the fact that almost every cottage, and indeed almost every monastery and church, is provided with loop-holes for defence against an invader, presents a singular admixture of consciousness to danger and of reliance on their own

* *Bulletin de la Société de Géographie*, April, 1865.
† UBICINI, *Les Serbes de Turquie*, pp. 148—150.
‡ *Travels in the Slavonic Provinces of Turkey*, vol. ii. p. 330, 2nd edition.
§ WILKINSON, vol. i. p. 407.

valour to repel hostile assaults. 'It is the knowledge of his own power to protect his family and his home which makes the Montenegrin live without dread of his many neighbouring enemies. The rugged barriers of rocky mountains that surround his village are his sentinels to prevent a surprise; and never did the Turks make an inroad upon Montenegro, whether in large or small numbers, without paying dearly for the injuries they inflicted.' *

Cetinje, the capital of Montenegro, may claim the distinction of being the smallest metropolis in the world. It stands in the midst of a sandy plain, about four thousand feet above the level of the sea, is shut in by precipitous rocks, and consists of little more than two streets, the longer one containing two or three poor inns and about sixty other houses, most of which rise to the dignity of one story, though scarcely any of them are better than those of a superior Highland village in Scotland. From this street a shorter one runs at right angles, containing the new residence of the Prince,† and opposite to it

---

* WILKINSON, vol. i. p. 410.

† 'I was struck with the good sense of the Prince who, reigning over a simple people of his own blood, is satisfied with a palace which does not even pretend to the privacy of a squire's mansion, but simply stands as the great house of an open village.'—FREEMAN.

the Government printing-office—the old half-Turkish house, built by Peter II., formerly occupied by the Vladika, and until recently tenanted by Prince Nicholas, but now chiefly used for a lodging for the guests of the Prince—and a house or two of the ordinary European type, inhabited by the senators during their residence in Cetinje, one of which, distinguished by a balcony, is occupied by the Vice-President of the Senate.

Thus much of the outside of the house. I shall best give an idea of the interior of a senatorial home in the capital of Montenegro by extracting from a letter, written immediately after a visit made by me to the Vice-President and to two of the other senators, a description of the apartment which I entered. 'On calling I was ushered up or at least walked up-stairs, which in two cases out of the three had no balustrades, into rooms which—I describe one—contained a bed, a chest of drawers, a table, a pier-glass, two cane-bottomed chairs, an arm-chair, a sofa, two painted trunks, and a German stove. The floor was partially covered with carpet. On the walls hung a picture of a saint with silver plating of the usual Byzantine or Russian type, large photographs, an engraved portrait of the late Emperor Nicholas, a splendid sabre, two or three pistols, a rifle, and a dress or two of Montenegrin manufacture, in fact, the court dress of the host. The senator, who was in his shirt-sleeves, helped me to raki, his son brought me a glass of water and cut up a fragrant melon, whilst I examined his library, which consisted of Millot's Universal History translated into Serbian, some religious works, and four or five collections of Montenegrin and other Serbian songs. There was no servant to be seen; but then we were not waited upon by the women, as we should have been in Serbia. For this is a custom derived from the Turk, and as Montenegro has never been held by the Turks long enough to introduce the customs of the East, female attendance is found less often at least in Montenegro than in Serbia. I do not mean to be understood to imply that a Montenegrin woman does not wait on her husband's guests, but only that she does so far less frequently than women in the neighbouring provinces.' *

A few paces from the old palace stands, on an abrupt ascent, the monastery of Cetinje, containing within it the cathedral of the diocese, the parish church of Cetinje, and the chapel of the monastery, built by the Vladika Danilo (1697—1737) on the

* *Good Words*, February, 1866.

ruins of a monastery founded in 1484 by Ivan Tzrnojivic, and partially destroyed in 1714. The small church itself was restored or rebuilt by the late Prince Danilo and the Princess Darinka on the occasion of their marriage. The building is capable of holding about 150 persons.* It contains the coffin of the Vladika Peter I., who died in 1830, and also the tombs of Prince Danilo and his brother, the Grand Voivode Mirko, father of the reigning Prince. The capitular, the parochial, and the monastic authorities are on a scale befitting the size of the capital, and consist of the Archbishop, the archimandrite of the convent, and one priest, who, in addition to being secretary to the Prince and Senate, was at the time of my visit, a few years since, also director of the

* Dr. Neale thus describes this building: 'The church is Romanesque and very small. It consists of apse, two little transepts, and nave. The apse arch is plain First Pointed; the nave is two bays, also First pointed. At the east end of the south transept lies the shrine of St. Peter: it is simply a bier with its hearse, over which a pall is thrown, there being no picture or other external symbol. The tower has a low pyramidal head. The façade of the monastery has three stages. The upper is a series of circular arches, supported on short circular piers, with square base and square cap; the second, of the same arches with square shafts; the third, of obtuse arches of contraction, rising out more than two feet from the ground. You enter the church at the right hand of this façade by a kind of vestibule additional to the south transept.'—*Notes on Dalmatia, Croatia, &c.*, p. 181.

printing-press of the Principality. If I add that he was not only director of the press, but also compositor, and occasionally pressman, that he compiled as well as printed the *Cetinje Almanac*, and wrote many of the poems which enliven its pages and adds to its popularity throughout Montenegro, I believe that I shall only assign to him some of his proper offices. Let not the reader smile; this concentration of duties is in keeping with the economy which reigns throughout the Black Mountains; and both Prince and people are fortunate in the holder of so many offices, the exercise of which recalls the times when the printing-press of England was sheltered within the cloisters of Westminster. Near the Prince's residence is the new boarding-school for girls, established a few years since at the expense of Prince Nicholas, and opposite to it a large but cheerless inn, erected for the accommodation of travellers from a distance. Near this inn is the small post-office of the Principality, from whence letters go to all parts of the world.*

In front of the old palace is a few yards of coarse grass shadowed by a carob-tree, under which the Prince dispenses justice, and idlers meet for

---

* 'Montenegro was a member of the Postal Union some months before France'—FREEMAN.

a gossip during the heat of the day. On a small patch of green adjoining lie some eight or nine pieces of artillery, of various sizes, the trophies of past wars with the Turks. A stone's throw from this, at the other end of the street, is a small triangular piece of ground, rising from which is a small oil-lamp, lighted on very dark nights. Here, under a plane-tree, round a well, which is opened twice a day for the supply of a stated quantity of water to the inhabitants, the traveller will find market women seated with baskets of eggs and vegetables for sale. The number of houses in 1858 was but sixteen, now it has upwards of sixty.* The entire population of the city is estimated at about six hundred residents, in addition to a small number of visitors, who at certain seasons of the year are attendant on the Senate, or may be waiting for the decision of the Prince in cases of appeal.

The route of the traveller who crosses Montenegro, either from the west and across the heights above

* UBICINI. 'The plain on which Cetinje is built forms an oblong, skirted by a little wood in the horizon. About the centre, but inclining towards the Cattaro side, some dozen white houses cluster around this fortified convent of the Vladikas, forming what in England would be called a small village or hamlet.'—*A Tour to Dalmatia and Montenegro*, by W. F. WINGFIELD, 1853.

Cattaro, or from the plain of Albania at the southeast, lies through the two most important villages in the Principality. Should he be travelling from the west, an hour and a half's ride from the top of the pass over Cattaro will bring him to Niegush, the seat of the powerful family or clan of Petrovic, the birth-place of Prince Nicholas, who belongs to this family, and the sanctuary of Montenegrin independence. This village was founded in the fifteenth century by refugees from the Herzegovina, who, under their Knes Petrovic, settled here, and gave to their new quarters the name of their native village. In 1697 one of the family, Daniel, or Danilo, became Vladika, since which time the ruler of Montenegro has been chosen or nominated from this family. This village, or rather cluster of seven villages, is scattered over a plain of about half a mile in extent.* As in the rest of the country, the chief care in building is not to encroach on land fit for cultivation; hence the houses are built on the rocky slope, and perched here and there, without regard to symmetry,

* 'Neigouchi, mentioné dans les livres et sur les cartes comme une des principales localités du Monténégro, désigne, non point une ville ou un bourg, mais un plémé composé de sept villages dont aucun ne porte le nom de Neigouchi.' —Ubicini, p. 150.

like grey blocks of stone scattered at random over a rocky plain. Formerly the houses, like those of the other villages throughout Montenegro, were thatched with straw or reeds, or were covered with wood shingles; these, however, are fast giving place to red tiles. Another improvement is visible in this village: the little cottages, with their one long room divided, and often imperfectly divided, between the family of the owner and the cattle which it possesses, are being superseded by houses built with a story above the ground-floor, and with separate accommodation for man and beast. Most travellers who have passed through Montenegro from Cattaro have mentioned the little inn or restaurant at this place, which was their first waiting-place. It will probably in a few years be so improved as hardly to be recognised. At present it is extremely characteristic. It consists of four small rooms, all in front, and two on each story. In one of the upper rooms the kitchen is placed, the floor being made of slabs of stone, supported on a frame of beech timber. The hearth is simply a square hole of some two feet diameter, sunk about six inches below the rest of the floor. The smoke—so much of it, at least, as escapes at all—is expected to escape through the proper hole in the roof. The other room on this floor is the sleeping apartment of the inn; it holds three beds. One half of the building is the Niegush inn, the other half is the village shop, very much on the modest scale of a shop in a small neglected village in England.

Each village of the cluster of villages which make up Niegush has its own humble church; and by the roadside is a school-house, built of good hewn stone by the present Prince, and serving for the whole of Nicgush. In front of the cottages are little irregular patches of garden ground, shaped as the rocky soil admits, and filled with the usual vegetables, potatoes, beans, melons of various kinds, radishes, cabbage, maize, capsicum, and horse-radish.

The other large village which the traveller passes if his route be through Montenegro from the south-east, a village which rises, indeed, almost to the dignity of a town, and approaches nearer to the character of the Dalmatian towns on the Adriatic shore than any other cluster of houses in Montenegro, stands near the Albanian frontier, and on the banks of the stream from which it has derived its own name, Rjeka. Built on the margin of the river, which sweeps in a semicircle at this spot, the houses rise to the unwonted height of two stories above the ground floor. The town is laid out in streets, and protected from inundation by an embankment with a parapet, built by Prince Danilo. A small bazaar and market-place, surrounded by a colonnade, lie behind the houses which face the river, near to which is a small house belonging to the Prince, and used by him as a hunting-box. Here most of the embroidery work for the dress of both sexes is executed; and the handsome features of the women engaged in this feminine task show what, but for their hard toil in the fields, the women of Montenegro would be. This town is the chief market in the Principality for muslin, linen, cloth, and other articles of dress. On the Saturday, when the market is held, the town presents a gay and animated appearance. It is attended by purchasers not only from other parts of Montenegro, but by many from Podgoritza and even Skodra. Rjeka has good and well-attended schools for boys and girls, and probably the best inn in the whole Principality.

About three-quarters of a mile from the town, at Obod, is the small manufactory of firearms, maintained by the Government. It is chiefly employed, however, in repairing and converting such rifles as have been purchased in Albania or captured from the Turks. Near this place may be seen some ruins, which are said to be those of the printing-house established here in the fifteenth century, but destroyed in one of the invasions of the Turks. At this town and in this printing-office the first book in the Slavonic language was printed, so that Rjeka is in this way the cradle of the literature of Russia, of Serbia, and of a large part of Austria. A copy of this book, the 'Osmo Glasnik,' is in the library of Prince Nicholas. It was printed in 7001 of the Greek era, corresponding to A.D. 1493. The river at this place is spanned by a bridge of three arches, built by Prince Danilo, which, having been destroyed by the Turks, was afterwards rebuilt by Prince Nicholas. The town labours under one disadvantage: the swamps near the river of the Rjeka render it unhealthy at certain times of the year.

In addition to the villages or towns of Cetinje, Niegush; and Rjeka, the most important village in Montenegro is that of Vir-Bazar, at the mouth of the Tzrnitza river, and in the nahia of the same name.

The most considerable and interesting relics of its old Roman rulers which are found in Montenegro are the remains of Dioclea, the birthplace of Diocletian, on the southern frontier of the Principality, and almost opposite the town of Podgoritza. This city was a place of considerable importance, not only in classical times, but far down into the period of the Serbian monarchy. It commands the only road from Albania to Bosnia, and stands at the southern entrance of the valley of Bielopavlic. It was built at the junction of the Zeta with the Moratcha, on a site of an irregular triangular form, having the Zeta on the south-west and the Moratcha on the south-east, and a rivulet—the Siralija—on the north-west. To the north of the city is the old Roman cemetery, and to the east the burial-place of Rogame, still used by the Montenegrins. The great gate of the city is on the north side; the defences which remain along the whole extent of the ancient city consist of a massive wall, strengthened at short intervals by square towers, the site being surrounded by a broad fosse on three sides. The two rivers which flow along the southern face of the city have eaten for themselves a course so far below the plain on which Dioclea stands that they add considerably to the strength of the fortifications.

From the time of its Roman builders down to the fourteenth century the name of this city repeatedly occurs in the annals of the Greek and Bulgarian wars. It was the seat, for a time, of an archbishop. In 1199 a synod was held here; and it is frequently mentioned as the residence of one or another of the ancient kings of Serbia. At present it consists of ruins only and of half-a-dozen cottages standing in the midst of vineyards and maize-grounds, which occupy the site of the imperial palace and the spacious basilica. Inscriptions and fragments of marble walls are found in great plenty, and some beautiful sculptured stones in a vault below the surface indicate the place of burial of the notabilities of the city. The bulk, however, of the marble which once covered the walls of the imperial residence has gone to the neighbouring cemetery. Here may be seen fragments of fluted columns cut into the requisite size and laid as tombstones. The covers and the bottoms of ancient stone coffins have been taken for the same purpose. Fine fragments of marble friezes, pagan altars, and in one place a magnificently carved console, serve the same purpose. The church round which the cemetery was first formed has for ages been in ruins; the churchyard, however, remains a favourite place for the burial of the villagers in the neighbourhood.

These ruins of a city once famous are almost wholly unknown to travellers, but are deserving of a careful examination. Coins, medals, terra cotta seals, intaglios, and other antiquities are often dug up in and around the ruins, but it is evident that still much remains underground. Prince Nicholas has a small collection of Roman imperial coins of silver which have mostly been found here.

Leaving the gates of this city the road runs northward along the narrow pass through which the river Zeta flows, and across a fine bridge of Roman or early Serbian work. Another bridge —the Hadzin Most, or pilgrim's bridge—which spans an arm of this river is a remarkable structure of one arch, and rises at so acute an angle that it is more usual for passengers to scramble across the bed of the stream than to pass over the bridge. Soon after crossing this bridge the traveller will begin to ascend the heights, near the top of which the monastery of Ostrog is situated. The monastery of Lower Ostrog—for there is a Higher and Lower Ostrog—is perched on a small plateau formed by the fall of a portion of the mountain behind it. Two or three immense boulders, resembling the bastions of a regular fortification, lie in front of the monastic buildings, and shut out the sight of them from below. There, wedged between two of these boulders, one of which has been converted into a small garden, and the earth which has accumulated in the crevices on its top planted with kitchen vegetables, stands the little church dedicated to the Holy Trinity, rebuilt in 1840, after being partially destroyed by the Turks. The apartments of the monks lie on the one side of this church, and on the other are the storehouse and rooms for the monastic servants. At some distance from the monastic buildings the present Prince has lately erected a long suite of rooms for the use of the pilgrims who on Trinity Sunday come in great numbers to Ostrog. Outside the gate of the monastery is another church—that of St. George—built in 1799; this, however, is seldom used; it seems to be the parochial church of the district, as distinguished from the monastic one.

Ostrog the higher is reached by a series of stepping-stones only affording room for one person to pass at the same time; it is scooped out of the face of a precipitous rock about two hundred feet below its summit. It is a hermitage rather than a monastery, except that the monk who inhabits it solaces himself by descending at times to enjoy the company of his brethren below. In the narrow dingy cell are a few Slavonic manuscripts and some early printed books from the press at Keiff. The small and singular chapel, in which the services of the Orthodox Church are sung daily, is a cavern in the live rock, with a lean-to roof of wooden slabs, under which it is just possible to stand upright. Its shape is as singular as everything else in the hermitage. The altar, placed on a natural shelf in the rock, stands north-east. Adjoining the chapel is the powder magazine belonging to the district. A spring gushing from the rock in this out-of-the-way place affords an unfailing supply of water. Near is a little garden of herbs, which is only accessible from the hermitage. A loopholed wall, two or three rifles, besides piles of stones, conveniently placed for hurling on the head of any intruder, make the place impregnable, whilst the garden and spring of water save it from many of the privations of a blockade. It is said never to have been entered by the Turks except for a short time during the war of 1862-3.[*]

On that occasion the Grand Voivode Mirko held

---

[*] Upwards of a hundred years ago Upper Ostrog 'was besieged by thirty thousand Turks for several months, when every effort was made to set fire to and destroy the fortress by lighted brands, and stones hurled from above; but all glanced off into the depth below, and though defended only by thirty men, the enemy was obliged to retire with immense loss. The Turks had laid waste everything in the neighbourhood with fire and sword; they had burnt the lower

this post with twenty-six men, and for eight days such cannon as the Turkish army had been able to drag to this point played from the heights opposite upon the living walls of this monastic fortress, but without making much impression upon the rock. Three or four assaults were easily repelled, with great loss to the assailants; and when provisions failed him Mirko withdrew with the loss of only one man, and reached Cetinje without molestation, in the face of thousands of hostile troops, who entered the hermitage only after the last of its defenders had retired.

The chapel of Upper Ostrog was hollowed out—I can hardly say built—by St. Basil, to whose memory it is dedicated, and was re-edified in 1774. His body, enclosed in a coffin, rests in the little choir of this miniature chapel. This St. Basil is not either of the theologians of that name, but a less distinguished local saint, formerly Metropolitan of the Herzegovina, who, tired out by the persecution of the Turks, took shelter in Montenegro some-

convent, which had already been destroyed nine times before, and they had advanced to a ledge of rocks a short distance to the south of the convent, when, stopped by an impassable precipice, they were all picked off by those within; and this last effort was the signal for the retreat.'—WILKINSON, vol. vi. p. 543.

where in the seventeenth century, and made this almost inaccessible spot his retreat. Here he died, and the little chapel or hermitage-monastery of Upper Ostrog was scooped out and consecrated to his memory soon after. His shrine, and indeed the two monasteries of Upper and Lower Ostrog, are held in such veneration that it is said that sometimes as many as twenty thousand pilgrims climb the heights and visit the churches there. These come from Bosnia, Albania, and the Herzegovina, as well as from all parts of Montenegro, and their great happiness is to be able to carry off little chippings of the rock for amulets. It is singular that the veneration for St. Basil is by no means confined to the Christians. The Bosnian Mahommedans esteem his shrine quite as highly as their Christian neighbours, and come in sickness and distress to pray before the coffin of the saint, and to entreat the prayers of St. Basil for themselves, their family, or friends. The tenacity with which the Bosnians, who were compelled to embrace Mahommedanism, cling to these and other observances of their old creed distinguish them from the rest of the worshippers of the false prophet. The annual offerings of the pilgrims are the chief source of revenue to these two monasteries, but in addition to these they possess some landed property in the neighbourhood of Dioclea, which is let out to tenants who return one-third of the produce by way of rent. A school has been built by Prince Nicholas near this monastery for the use of the surrounding villages.

CHAPTER V.

POPULATION—MILITARY FORCES—TACTICS.

It is not easy to arrive at any satisfactory conclusion as to the population of Montenegro in past times, nor consequently to estimate with precision the rate of its increase. The estimates made by travellers in their transit across the Principality are generally vague and almost worthless, whilst the alterations of the frontier-line of Montenegro at different periods of its history diminishes the value even of these vague estimates.

In the seventeenth century (1614) Mariano Bolizza, a Venetian nobleman residing at Cattaro, in his 'Relatione,' computed that Montenegro contained 90 villages, 3,524 houses or families, and 8,027 fighting-men.* In 1800, according to M. Cyprien Robert, the population of Montenegro, with

---

* ' Montenegro è constituta da novanta villagi, che fanno case tre mille cinquecento vintiquattro, può far gente armata da combatter otto mille vinti sette, frà quali vi possono esser mille archebuggieri; il resto spada, targa e giavarina.'

the recent addition of the Berda, only reached about 50,000—an estimate confirmed by the researches of Colonel Vialla. The same writer states that, according to the census of 1812, the population was 53,168, and the number of men bearing arms and available in time of war to be 13,292. In 1825 the population had increased to 75,000, and the military array to 15,000; and fifteen years later, in 1835, the population was believed to be 100,000. In 1846 it was estimated that the numbers of the Montenegrins had reached 11,700 families, with a military strength of 20,000 combatants, and a presumed total of 120,000 individuals; and about twenty years later, in 1864, the official return, according to the *Cetinje Almanac* of that date, gives 196,238 as the number of people belonging to the Principality.* Supposing the estimate made in 1800 to be correct, the population has doubled itself twice during the present century, that is to say,

* Of these 99,889 were males and 96,349 females. These were thus distributed:—

Katunska Nahia	63,738
Rjetska Nahia	26,097
Tzrnitza Nahia	28,269
Liechanska Nahia	15,367
The four Berda	62,767
Giving a total of	196,238

(The *Gorlitza.* Cetinje, 1865.)

once in about thirty years—a much higher rate of increase than that of any of the adjoining Christian provinces of Turkey.*

As the sterility of the rocky soil and the absence of any outlets for their industry prevent an increasing population from finding scope for their energies in their own country, or even permit of their finding the means of subsistence, a large number are yearly compelled to emigrate to various surrounding countries; and the gardens on the Bosphorus, the vegetable markets of Constantinople and of the towns of Asia Minor, are supplied by Montenegrin gardeners—who, however, are enrolled on the books of the Principality, and return to their respective villages at fixed intervals, to be exercised and mustered with the effective strength of the community.† In time of war, as at present, these

---

* The births in 1864 were 6,577; the deaths, 3,938 (UBICINI). I am unable to supply later figures. In answer to my inquiries for such information I received from Cetinje, while these pages were passing through the press, the characteristic reply: 'As to the statistics you require, I am sorry to be quite unable to satisfy you. The events of the late years have given so much to do to everybody on urgent every-day business, that no time was left to the very few officials who have all the work to do themselves to compile statistics.'

† As Montenegro at the best of times barely furnishes food for its people, an unfavourable harvest causes famine, starva-

men throw up their occupations abroad and flock back to their native country. These men and their families are no doubt included in the census returns of Montenegro together with the stated inhabitants. At present the Montenegrins may be safely estimated to number about 220,000.

The proportion of men, able, ready, and expected to bear arms in case of war—for these terms are convertible—is higher in Montenegro than in other countries. Age claims no exemption, and familiarity with arms from, and indeed in, the cradle, makes its sons available at a far earlier age than elsewhere. In the war with Turkey in 1862 'corpses of children under fourteen years of age were frequently reported as found among the slain.'* The present captain of Niegush, Juro Petrovic, narrowly escaped with his life from a battle-field at the age of twelve, and a recent writer relates that on the occasion, a few years ago, of a review at Cetinje, Prince Nicholas, remarking a young man terribly scarred, asked him how he had met with his accident, on which the soldier

tion, and those diseases which follow upon insufficient food. To this Colonel Vialla attributes in great measure the slow increase of the population during the last century (*Voyage Historique*, t. i. p. 88).

* *Travels in the Slavonic Provinces of Turkey*, by MISSES IRBY and MUIR MACKENZIE, vol. ii. p. 199, 2nd edition.

replied, 'I was wounded in the war under Mirko.' 'How old,' said the Prince, 'could you have been? you are scarce a man yet.' 'I was thirteen,' said the young hero quietly.*

So predominant are the ideas of military service, so certain the necessity of being called upon to take up arms in defence of his country, that at his baptism the butt of a pistol is put to the child's mouth for him to kiss, and the pistol itself placed in his cradle as naturally as with us a coral is given to an infant for a plaything. Boys of six or seven years old are indulged with a dagger, and at ten may be seen strutting about with a rifle suitable to their age. One favourite toast at the baptism of a boy is, 'May he not die in his bed;' and no taunt goes home so surely to a Montenegrin's heart as this, 'Your forefathers all died in their beds.' †

Nor is the obligation of military service confined to the laity. So far from holy orders hindering any one from rendering active service in the field, in many districts the village pastor, who leads the devotions of his people in peace, approves himself an able captain

* *Le Monténégro Contemporain,* p. 132.
† VIALLA DE SOMMIÈRES, *Voyage Historique,* &c., t. i. p. 102. *Researches on the Danube and the Adriatic,* by A. A. PATON, vol. i. p. 180. *Turcs et Monténégrins,* par F. LENORMANT p. xvi.

in times of danger. Like the rest of the Montenegrins, the priests carry arms, and 'are generally good "heroes," the first at a gathering, the leaders of their flocks in war.' The instinct of self-preservation, and the half-religious character of their wars with the Turks—for all the wars of the Montenegrins hitherto have been defensive—excuse or even make a virtue of what would be regarded as an impropriety in other civilised communities. Indeed, until the separation of the ecclesiastical and civil functions of the ruler, the Prince-Bishop, like many of the German and even some English bishops in the Middle Ages, led his subjects into the field; and the last two predecessors of Prince Danilo were men who had earned the respect of their people, not only by their administrative ability in Church and State, but also for their physical powers and martial skill. In fact, Montenegro is an armed camp, even more than a nation in which a division of duties and labour can be recognised—a camp girded by the almost inaccessible rampart which nature has thrown up in front of the Albanian plain, and manned by soldiers accustomed to confront danger from infancy, and to regard death in the battle-field as their special privilege and glory.* For if 36,000 men, or more

* 'A part quelques couvents, dont ils ont pris à tâche de

than one-fourth of the male population, can be depended upon to obey the summons of their Prince to arms, a larger number even than this would, not need to be called upon but would, hasten unbidden to hurl back invasions from their mountain homes. Even this number of men, however, by no means represents the armed force which would resist the advance of a Turkish army, and guard the rugged defiles which open upon their plains.* Feeble old age vindicates its right to share in the fray, and even cripples at such times compel their neighbours to carry them to the post of danger, so that from the rocks they may fire upon the invaders.†
But not only men, the girls and women, who, to say the least, share with their brothers and husbands in

bâtir solidement les murs, on ne découvrirait pas dans leur principauté un travail de fortification. La nature a été gratuitement elle-même leur Vauban. La nature leur a fait un cercle de remparts, une enceinte continue qui n'exigent aucuns frais de réparation.'—MARMIER, t. ii. p. 105.

* The ordinary proportion of males in a population between the ages of seventeen and sixty is estimated at 7-25th of the whole.

† LENORMANT. 'During the war with the Turks in 1796, Giuro Lottocich was confined to his bed by a broken leg, but hearing of the battle, in which Kara Mahmoud (Bushullia) was defeated and slain, he insisted upon being carried out to a rock, from whence he could fire on the enemy, which, in spite of every remonstrance, he continued to do, supported against a rock, for three whole hours; and when

the labours of agriculture, claim also the right to share with them the toils and dangers of war; and whilst the past history of this people abound in instances of female heroism, the national songs which have had so large a share in moulding the Montenegrin character, have preserved the memory, and hold up to imitation the deeds of the wife who has not only hurried to and fro with food for her husband engaged in the thick of the fight, but has stood by his side through the long day of conflict, has loaded his rifle, has borne his banner in the field, and has even aided him, with sword in hand, in defending their common country.*· 'Pity she is not a boy, she would be a second Mirko,' was a remark often made in admiration of the sister of Prince Nicholas,

---

they told him of the victory, he exclaimed, "It is time, indeed, for I have no more cartridges, and I should have died of rage if I had been forced to surrender." '—WILKINSON, vol. i. p. 408.

* 'Le chiffre que nous avons indiqué n'est que celui des combattants toujours prêts à entrer en campagne, et à porter, si les circonstances y sont favorables, la guerre sur le territoire ennemi; mais qu'un danger sérieux menace le pays, qu'une armée turque s'avance pour le réduire, la première balle qui frappera les rochers de Tsernogore en fera sortir de tous côtés des bras et des carbines; femmes, vieillards, enfants, soutiendront les hommes faits la défense nationale. Au lieu de 35,000 guerriers, la montagne noire en comptera ce jour-là 100,000.'—LENORMANT.

who, whenever her father would suffer it, followed him to the war.

'The finest story of a fair warrior in Montenegro was told us by one of her fellow combatants, who seemed truly proud of his countrywoman. Her husband was a standard-bearer. He fell in battle, and was succeeded in office by the eldest of his grown-up sons. That son fell, and was followed by a second, and he in turn by a third. The woman's fourth and last son was still a child, so she shouldered the banner herself, saying, "I will bear it till my son be grown."'*

Whilst, however, the military force of Montenegro is in this way out of all proportion to the number of its inhabitants, its army, in the technical term of the word, can hardly be said to have any existence, or at least is the smallest in the world. Up to the year 1853 the army of Montenegro was only the armed array of the inhabitants, self-disciplined, and kept in a continual state of efficiency by the incessant wars on the frontier. A hundred men (*perianiks*), chosen from the various districts of Montenegro, acted, as they still act, as guards to the Prince and as messengers to the court. About

* *Travels in the Slavonic Provinces of Turkey*, vol. ii. p. 200, 2nd edition.

four hundred others (*pandours*) are charged with the preservation of the peace within the various divisions of the country, and act as police officers. These receive a small, almost nominal, pay, and gain their livelihood, as almost every one else in the Principality, by tilling their rood or bit of land. The age when military service is expected is fixed at seventeen; though, as I have already shown, it practically commences much earlier: it extends legally to fifty, but in fact it is limited only by extreme old age and decrepitude.

None of the soldiers receive pay unless those selected as the Prince's guards or as *pandours;* these have a small, almost nominal, pay. When called out for active service all provide their own provisions. When their services are required by actual or prospective hostilities, with the summons to the field is indicated the probable duration of the expedition to which they are summoned, so that they may be able to bring with them the requisite quantity of food. The contingent of each *nahia* is commanded by its own *voivode*. The soldiers of each *pleme* have their own *capetan*, under whom are the *stotinatch*, a centurion commanding fifty houses, or, estimating two soldiers to each house, a body of one hundred men, and subordinate to these a number of decurions (*decetcharj*), each commanding five houses or ten men. Each tribe has its own banner. The standard of Montenegro is tricoloured, as the French, but ranged in horizontal bands. These, according to the Montenegrins represent faith (blue), hope (white), and charity (red).* The ancient arms of the Principality are the double-headed eagle of Byzantium, with a lion passant on a kind of escutcheon of pretence. These arms, stamped on a medal with the significant motto of *Viera zncoboda za hrabrost* ('Faith and freedom the reward of valour'), are given by the Prince to those who distinguish themselves in battle with the Turk.

The captains and standard-bearers of the various districts have the whole charge of the military array of their respective territories, and the zeal and training of the people supply all deficiencies. Upwards of 10,000 men can be assembled at any point of the frontier within twelve hours of the first intimation of danger, and twenty-four hours are sufficient to concentrate almost the whole male population above the age of fourteen. These are all active skirmishers, efficient marksmen, and excellently suited for such irregular warfare as their country alone admits of. Being inured to hardships

* LENORMANT.

and privations, they perform, without fatigue and in high spirits, very long and forced marches. They leap over wide ditches, supporting themselves on their long rifles, and pass over precipices where bridges would be absolutely requisite for any other kind of troops, and they climb the steepest rocks with the greatest facility; they also bear, with the utmost patience, hunger, thirst, and every kind of privation. When the enemy is defeated and retiring, they pursue him with such rapidity that they supply the want of cavalry, which it is impossible to employ in their mountainous country.*

The commissariat of these troops is of the simplest description, being a small loaf of bread, a cheese, some garlic, a little brandy. An old garment and two pairs of sandals made of raw hide form all the equipment of the Montenegrins. On their march they disdain to seek any shelter from rain or cold. In rainy weather the Montenegrin wraps around his head, or more frequently round his rifle, the *strooka*,† or shawl of coarse cloth, lies down on the ground, and, putting his rifle under him, sleeps comfortably. Three or four hours of repose are quite sufficient for

---

* M. BRONIEWSKI in Count V. Krasinski's *Montenegro and the Slavonians of Turkey.*

† MARMIER.

his rest, and the remainder of his time is occupied in constant exertion. In accordance with their usual tactics, if in great force they conceal themselves in ravines, sending out a small number of marksmen, who, by retreating, lead the enemy into the ambuscade. When they have surrounded their foes, on the slightest appearance of disorder in their ranks, they throw aside their rifles, and rush to the attack with their handgars, and rely upon their personal strength and individual bravery, in which they have almost always the advantage of their enemies. When their numbers are too small to justify their advancing in the open field, they seize positions amid inaccessible rocks, and harass their foes with a deadly fire, which they are unable to return with any effect. A hole, a stone, or the trunk of a tree offers them a cover from their enemy. As they usually fire in a prostrate position, they are seldom hit in these encounters, whilst their rapid and sure shots carry destruction into the ranks of the enemy. Their history is full of well-attested but almost incredible exploits done in these conflicts. It is of frequent occurrence that whilst their own number may not have reached a tenth of their opponents, the number of these opponents which they have left dead on the field have exceeded that of the whole number of

Montenegrin combatants. These levies resemble, in short, the Highlanders of a century ago, and their military array and accoutrements carry us back to the days of Prince Charles Edward and to the bands which fought under his standard at Prestons-pans and Culloden.

CHAPTER VI.

PRESENT MILITARY ORGANIZATION.

In the previous chapter we have seen what the military characteristics of these people are. To these rather than to any scientific organization they have owed the preservation of their independence in past times. So long as the Turkish armies were drilled after the ancient rules of military tactics, and were armed with the old-fashioned weapons in use during the European war which closed in 1815, individual courage sufficed the Montenegrins without any great amount of military discipline or organization. With the change of tactics and with the introduction of new arms it was evident, however, that Montenegro would have to modify its old military system, and to furnish its soldiery with improved weapons of war. The accession of Danilo, in 1851, the first secular prince since the beginning of the sixteenth century, was signalised not only by a new code of civil laws for the Principality, but also with the commencement of a reform of its military forces. Attention was now directed to military science, of which hitherto there had been but little account in Montenegro, and the beneficial results were evident in the war of 1853.

In 1862, however, before any considerable step could be taken in this direction, the Montenegrin forces, untaught to act in large bodies, and armed with the old muzzle-loading rifle, were called upon to encounter troops disciplined after the most approved modern system of tactics, led by a renegade Serb from Austria, and armed with weapons of precision. These were advantages on the side of the Turks which no courage on the part of the Montenegrins could overcome. The losses of the Montenegrins, accordingly, were greater in this war than at any previous time. It was evident, if their cherished independence was much longer to be a possession, science must come to the aid of courage. The people were quick to learn the lesson, and had a prince who knew how to put it to a practical use. Prince Danilo and his brother, the Grand Voivode Mirko, had already directed their attention to the systematic organization of the armed array of the country. Little, however, had been done to supply the army with new and efficient weapons at the time of the death of Danilo. Indeed the great European powers had hardly done more than commence this work, and had not come to any decision as to the best weapon for their troops. The campaign, however, of 1862 satisfied the present Prince, who found himself the inheritor of a war with veteran Turkish troops drilled by English officers, and fresh from the campaign in the Crimea, that it was necessary to improve the military organization of the Principality.* As soon as peace was established, the task of arming the nation with new weapons was seriously undertaken.

To procure a sufficient quantity of such arms entailed an expense which it seemed, at first, that Montenegro could not bear. Patriotism and energy, however, furnished the means. With the consent of the Imperial Government of France, a lottery was established in Paris, and the proceeds, augmented by a gift of money from the Emperor Napoleon, were devoted to the purchase of twelve thousand Minié rifles, and these, as soon as they reached Cetinje,

---

* Among more substantial fruit of the victory at Grahova, in 1858, was a quantity of medals given by the English Government to the men of the Turkish contingent for bravery in the Crimean campaign. These medals are now at Cetinje.

were served out to the most active soldiers and best marksmen. To the sum thus obtained was added a seasonable gift from Prince Michel of Serbia, and a donation of about £1,500 made by a patriotic Serb, and these together were devoted to the purchase of five hundred rifles, five hundred swords, and paper for a million of cartridges for the new rifles.

As the geographical position of Montenegro allowed Austria to prevent at any time the introduction of arms into the country, and the power of doing so was often exercised by the Imperial Government, and always at a time when such arms were most needed, it was necessary that the means of manufacturing and repairing firearms should exist in Montenegro itself, and that workmen should be taught how to convert the old weapons, taken from time to time from the Turks or purchased in Albania, into modern firearms, as well as how to manufacture rifles of an improved pattern, and how to make the cartridges necessary for such new rifles Hitherto this had been done to so small an extent at the little arsenal near Rjeka, as to make the Montenegrins almost wholly dependent upon a foreign supply. To meet this necessity Prince Michel of Serbia sent, in 1866, a skilful workman from Belgrade, under whose superintendence the old armoury at Obod was brought to a state of efficiency, and a number of Montenegrins instructed how to convert the old muzzle-loading weapons into breech-loading rifles. At the request of Prince Nicholas, the help thus afforded by the Prince of Serbia was supplemented by the arrival of three artillerists, who commenced a foundry for cannon near Cetinje. In this little arsenal is stored up a reserve of arms, of powder, and of the munitions of war. A manufactory for the making of cartridges for the new rifles was next established at the extremity of the plain in which Cetinje stands. This has succeeded so well, that when the present war commenced the storehouses contained a stock sufficient to allow of four hundred cartridges being served out to each man under arms.

In addition to the artillery officers and instructors furnished by Prince Michel from Belgrade, a trumpeter was sent in order to teach the Montenegrin troops the various signals employed in the Serbian army, and to enable them to communicate at a greater distance than before. Hitherto their only means had been the human voice. In 1869 two thousand needle-guns were added to the stock of warlike materials.

As soon as these expensive works were achieved, in 1870, the scientific organization of the Montene-

H

grin peasantry was undertaken. At present the army is thus organized and equipped.

The military array of Montenegro, the men between the ages of seventeen and sixty, consists of two divisions, each of which contains 10,000 men, supported by a battery of mountain artillery. Each division is divided into two brigades, each brigade being composed of five battalions, four of which are armed with the Minié rifle, and the remaining battalion of picked marksmen with the needle-gun. Every battalion is composed of eight companies, the battalion being commanded by a major and the various companies by a captain. Every company consists of ninety men rank and file, ten corporals, a trumpeter, an ensign, two subalterns, and the captain. Thus the company is of the strength of 105 men, while the whole battalion contains 842 men.

The army is thus armed: 12,000 men are supplied with the Minié rifles, rather more than 3,000 have the needle-gun, about 1,000 men have old rifles converted into breechloaders, and the remainder are still armed with the old Albanian rifle, which is loaded at the muzzle. The mountain artillery attached to each brigade is regulated after the Swiss model, and consists of four guns, served by forty-eight men, with three officers. The various nahias are called upon to furnish battalions in proportion to the number of their population. The strength of these battalions are equal to most ordinary regiments. They can seldom, however, act in a body. The nature of the ground in most parts of Montenegro would prevent this. This gives to the companies which compose the battalions a greater degree of independent action, and makes them of greater importance.

The staff of the army consists of the Prince, who is the commander-in-chief. He is assisted in this command by a chief of the staff and by a certain number of aides-de-camp. Each of the divisions of the army is under the charge of a voivode as general of division, and under him are two voivodes as generals of brigades. All these officers are appointed by the Prince. The selection of the officers of a lower grade rests with these general officers.

The Prince supplies to the soldier the rifle which he uses in action and such cartridges as he may require. He gives nothing more. No Montenegrin receives pay for his services in the field. The soldiers are summoned to fight for their homes and their common country, and this it is their duty to do as much as it is that of the Prince.* They have no

* The captain receives a gratuity of about four pounds a

special uniform beyond the distinctive national dress which all wear. They move without ambulances. They are not hampered with tents. They need no baggage waggons since they have no baggage. There is no commissariat required to supply them with food, nor has any one the duty assigned to him of serving them with ammunition. Their war being one of defence, they are always within reach of their homes; and just as with us the wife or child brings to the harvest field the food which the reapers require, so day by day the wife seeks her husband on the battle-field, and supplies him with the food which she has prepared for him, or brings to him from the public stores the powder which he requires. If the course of the war carries him beyond the frontier of Montenegro, a little maize bread, washed down by water from the running stream, satisfies the wants of the soldier until he is again within reach of home. No arrangements can be more simple. A War Office clerk would despair in such an absence of all commissariat provisions. Yet these arrangements have enabled the Montenegrin peasant soldier to check the advance of the most dis-

year. This small sum is not given as a payment for services but in order to meet certain expenses to which they are subjected in the fulfilment of their military duties.

ciplined armies, and effectually to guard the independence of his country.

As all their wars have strictly been wars of defence, and as no campaign beyond the bounds of their own rugged homes has been contemplated, they have not employed cavalry for some three hundred years or more, that is since they lost possession of the plain which stretches from the banks of the Moratcha to the southern shore of the Lake Skodra. Cavalry could not act in Montenegro and hardly in the Berda, and even if it were possible for such an arm of the military service to be of use, few of these soldiers could maintain a horse. Twenty pounds a year is beyond the means of all save a few of the large landowners; and their estates, as I have already mentioned, are not large enough to enable them to spend so much money uselessly. The Montenegrin army therfore consists entirely of infantry and artillery.

They have no fortresses to defend. No semblance of blockhouse or fortification of the humblest description exists in Montenegro. Their whole country is one natural fortress—they need no other.*

The organization of the Montenegrin army aims at

* For the details of the new military organisation of Montenegro I am chiefly indebted to the authors of *Le Monténégro Contemporain.*

obtaining the advantage of discipline and the power of combined action without fettering too much the individual action of the soldier. On this individuality the ultimate reliance is still placed. The new discipline is but supplementary to the long-tried tactics which have proved so effective in their mountain warfare of four centuries. Nor, again, does the enrolment of the able-bodied men in two divisions in any way exclude the very efficient help which in a conflict amid the rocks of their homes, old men, boys, and women yet still hasten to give.*

* 'Ce qui caractérise surtout le Monténégrin comme guerrier, et ce qui lui conserve sa supériorité sur toute espèce de soldats européens, c'est le sentiment de son individualité, l'orgueil de cette indépendance même avec laquelle il accomplit les actes de bravoure les plus audacieux et quelquefois même les plus inconsidérés. Le gouvernement ne devra donc point, en exagérant sa tendance actuelle, chercher à substituer complètement l'action du commandement à l'initiative particulière.'—*Le Monténégro Contemporain*, p. 452.

CHAPTER VII.

PHYSICAL CHARACTERS—LONGEVITY—DRESS— COTTAGES—HOME LIFE.

THEIR life, passed in the pure mountain air, the necessity of being always under arms, and always, therefore, in activity, together with the frugality of their homes, save the Montenegrins from many of the diseases of our more artificial civilisation. They possess in general robust health, the aid of the physician and the surgeon is rarely required, since in no country are gun-shot and sabre wounds so speedily healed as among these mountains. Instances of greatly prolonged life are common among the peasantry. Colonel Vialla de Sommières * mentions a family he saw in the village of Schiéclic, near Niegush, which included in its living members six generations. Its aged patriarch was one hundred and seventeen years old, his son was one hundred,

* *Voyage Historique et Politique au Monténégro*, t. i. p. 123.

his grandson eighty-two, and his great-grandson sixty years old; the son of this great-grandson was forty-three years old; he had a son aged twenty-one, who was the father of a two-years-old child.

These descendants down to the great-great-grandchildren inhabited the same house as the father of their great-great-grandfather. This would be more incredible were it not for the fact that the Montegrins generally marry very early. This instance of longevity is, however, in keeping with the reputation for long life which was enjoyed by the people of these countries in old time.*

The acuteness of their hearing rivals that of the North American Indians, and the quickness of their eye enables them to see at immense distances, and to adjust their rifles without artificial aid. Short-sightedness is almost unknown among these mountaineers.† Intermittent fevers, especially in the neighbourhood of Rjeka, rheumatism, scrofula, and dysentery in one form or another, are the chief maladies of the country, and among females, but more rarely, cases of consumption occur. In 1867 Montenegro was visited with a very severe attack

* PLINY, vii. 48. WILKINSON, vol. i., p. 419.
† *Le Monténégro Contemporain*, p. 130.

of cholera, which carried off a large number of the inhabitants.

In stature the men are athletic, and well-proportioned, though many of them, especially in the districts of Tzrnitza and Bielopavlic, are unusually tall; their mien is warlike, and their tread firm, like that of mountaineers in general. A recent ruler of Montenegro was six feet eight inches in height, and instances of men who reach six feet six inches are far from uncommon. Their frame is sinewy and lithe. Their eyes are large and strikingly intelligent and animated, though without the fierce expression of the Turks.* Their nose is short and moderately aquiline or straight; their mouth and chin are firmly moulded; their forehead is somewhat square; and whilst most of them wear the moustache, all except their clergy shave their beards. Their complexion, from exposure, is usually of a sun-burnt red, and their hair mostly brown. Intermingled, however, with people of this Serb type are those who have features of a more classical character, and some writers have seen in these the remains of the Greek and Roman colonies which were displaced by the first Slav immigrants.

* SIR GARDNER WILKINSON, vol. i. p. 481. *Travels in South Slavonic Countries*, vol. ii. p. 222.

The women are scarcely of middle height, thickset, with fair but weather-beaten complexions, and generally with harsh features, the result of early toil, which robs them of the beauty of early life. Those of the Berda are usually blonde, whilst those of Montenegro proper are distinguished for their black hair and dark complexion. In manners, both men and women have a natural unembarrassed air, and all travellers agree in praising their intelligence. Their food is as simple as their mode of living is hardy and primitive, and to this the general good health of these mountaineers must be attributed. Their usual food consists of coarse unleavened bread made of Indian corn, *polenta*, cheese, milk, and vegetables. Meat and fish are rarely eaten, except on great occasions, and poultry seldom appears on the table, except when the visit of a stranger calls them to exert their hospitality. They are fond of wine, though few are able to drink it because of the expense; on some of the greater festivals, however, such as Easter, Christmas, or the feast-day of St. Elias, they indulge their taste in this respect. Brandy and spirituous liquors in general are in esteem, but their poverty fortunately prevents their using them, except when a visit to Cattaro enables them to obtain the luxury at a cheap rate.

Of the dress of these people Lady Strangford, describing the dress of the Prince and of the men in general, says:—

'The Montenegrin custom is the handsomest and most graceful I have seen in any country. The Prince wore dark-blue cloth pantaloons, cut in the square style, very full and wide, gathered in at the knee, with scarlet garters; a Damascus silk scarf round the loins, and at his waist a huge crimson leather band, in which his arms are placed; the Prince, however, is the only man who carries none at home. The scarlet waistcoat, embroidered and buttoned with gold, is half concealed by a closely fitting tunic of white cloth, also richly embroidered in gold; the full court dress is the same, only that the tunic is then worn of green. Sometimes fur edgings are added, and all the gentlemen about the court have rows of large silver buttons sewn so thickly on the front of the tunic as quite to conceal the cloth, and to give the appearance of armour; while some had enormous shoulder-pieces of solid silver covered with bosses, completely covering the head and shoulders. The cap is of fur, with a *panache* of white cloth, embroidered and tasselled, hanging down at one side; this is in war, or in travelling, or in winter; in summer, or at home, the Montenegrin wears a peculiar pork-pie cap, with a black silk border and a scarlet centre. All the Montenegrins wear embroidered leggings. The Prince alone wears high leather boots. He wore gloves, as did every one at court, constantly.

'The dress of the peasants is made more or less in the same form, of commoner materials. All of these add, for cold and rainy weather, a thick cloak, called the *strooka*, which is made of undyed wool, coarsely spun in long frills, so as closely to resemble an untanned sheepskin.'*

In the description of the dress of Prince Nicholas, which differs but little save in the quality of the material from that worn by Montenegrins in general, there is one noticeable omission. Except in actual warfare the Prince never, or but very seldom, carries weapons: his people are rarely without them. The sash and leathern girdle round their waist is rarely without a brace of pistols, and if a peasant walks beyond the bounds of his own village he has usually a long rifle swinging behind him. The arms assumed in boyhood are never laid aside.†

---

* *The Eastern Shores of the Adriatic*, pp. 146, 147.

† 'Ici ne dépose rien de les instruments de guerre. Ici les armes font partie essentielle du vêtement. On peut bien n'avoir qu'une chemise éraillée et un pantalon en loques, mais quelle honte si on ne pouvait étaler sur sa

Of the people in general Sir Gardner Wilkinson says:—

'They wear a white or yellow cloth frock, reaching almost to the knees, secured by a sash round the waist; under it is a red cloth vest, and over it a red or green jacket without sleeves, both richly embroidered; and the whole covered with a jacket bordered with fur.

'The female dress consists of a frock or pelisse of white cloth, without sleeves, and open in front, like that of the men, but much longer, reaching nearly to the ankles, and trimmed with various devices in braiding, or coloured cloth, and tassels, and in front are several gold ornaments.'*

Though there is much the same relative distinction between the farmhouses of the larger proprietors of twenty or thirty acres of arable land and the cottage of the owner of two acres of ground, as between the house of a small farmer and of a labourer in England, yet, as the larger proprietors are few in number, and poverty is the lot of the bulk of the people of Montenegro, the description of an ordinary cottage will give a tolerably correct idea of the habits

poitrine deux crosses de pistolet et la poignée d'un glaive.'— MARMIER, t. ii. p. 115.

* *Dalmatia and Montenegro*, vol. ii. pp. 152, 153.

and mode of life prevalent throughout the Principality. I therefore borrow from my note-book a sketch of a Montenegrin cottage:—

'After about six hours' ride we found ourselves in the middle of the little village of Gradatz. On one side of the road was a threshing-floor, raised about ten feet above the pathway, and resting on large uncemented stones. The space below the floor was used as a storehouse for straw and maize stalks. The threshing-floor itself, like all others throughout Montenegro, was well cemented and finished with care, and surrounded by a wall of about two feet in height. A white mulberry-tree in the centre of the road flung its shade over the threshing-floor. On the other side of the way was a garden wall of uncemented stones, flecked with lichens and half-covered with blackberry-bushes. Inside the wall a pigsty and another mulberry-tree filled up the little court. The house itself was but one apartment, partially divided in the centre by hurdles. It had two doors in front, so that it had the appearance of two small houses instead of one large one, and each end was lighted by a small unglazed window or loophole. Behind, the roof of thatch, kept down by means of bands and large stones, rested on the live rock. In front, the wall was of hewn, cemented stone, with here and there a loophole for defence. In the part which I first entered, one or two logs and a wooden chair were all the ostensible seats; others, however, could be extemporised out of the boxes, clumps of wood, and large stones which lay on the earthen floor. Overhead were a few rafters, not, however, to support a ceiling, for there was none, but ranged from wall to wall as a convenient means of supplying the place of cupboards. From these rafters hung strings of onions, a ham or two, some salted fish, and two or three sheets of paper, covered with silkworms' eggs hung up for hatching. Two or three earthen jars for water, a wooden bicker for milk, a coarse woollen rug, a child's cradle of primitive construction, a couple of reaping-hooks, a heavy horse-pistol and a rifle, were all visible through the dingy atmosphere. On one of the logs sat a woman nursing her infant, two or three other children crowded behind their mother and peered over her shoulder with awe and astonishment at the strangers. In another part of the room, stretched at full length in a sound sleep, was a girl of some fifteen years, and at her feet lay a young calf in apparently the same state of unconsciousness, whilst a couple of dogs contested with the children the occupancy of the floor. Behind the hurdle other members of the family had collected, to watch our movements from a safe distance. This apartment contained the rough boards on which the bedding of the various members of the family could be laid. A mass of rugs and other furniture for beds occupied one corner, and firewood was heaped up in another. On a fire in the centre of the cottage was placed a pot, the steam from which announced that preparation for dinner was going on. What else there might be I could not see, as the smoke from the beech logs obscured the room before it escaped from the regular outlets in the roof, as there was no chimney. It was just such a picture as Sir Walter Scott has left us of a Highland cottage of the last century, or, indeed, such as several estates in Scotland can show even at the present day. The heaps of maize for man and pig, the mulberry-tree, the fig-branches trailing over the wall, the vine heavy with purple clusters of grapes, and the hedges of pomegranate bushes on fire with scarlet blossoms, were southern, and gave a local colouring to the scene; but, apart from these, it was easy to imagine oneself in some unfrequented spot, at a distance from railways, in the northern part of Great Britain.'*

Monsieur Lenormant, who lived for several years

---

* *Good Words*, September, 1866.

in the country, has drawn from the life a picture of the home occupations of a Montenegrin's family, which will best convey to the reader a notion of the life of peaceful pastoral simplicity of these highland warriors. Let us lift the latch with him and look around the house, which may be taken as a fair type of a cottage home in the mountains.

An aged couple, bent with years and toil, are the sole occupants of the cottage, except some infants too young for labour, who are playing on the floor. The long flaxen hair and light blue eyes of the children speak of a northern race. The aged couple are the grandparents—often the great-grandparents—to whom all pay the utmost deference—not only their own children, but their grandchildren and their children; the sons-in-law and the daughters-in-law submit to their authority. Their white hair tells of their great age. The old man is no longer reckoned in the military strength of the celo to which he belongs, and wounds received in past wars have had their share in making him less active. But though no longer compelled to take the field, let but the sound of the Turkish drum be heard in the valley where he lives, and he will be seen hurrying to defend their home, and will be found fighting, surrounded by his

I

children and grandchildren. At present the sole occupation of himself and his wife is the care of the infants. Whilst smoking around the fire he spends his time in carving some pieces of wood intended for the use and decoration of the cottage; she employs herself in repairing the tattered garments of the household, and in watching the children at their sports.

And now the sun, the only clock which is known to these mountaineers, the only clock found in all Montenegro, except at Cetinje or at Ostrug, tells that the day is declining.* The hour for the family supper is drawing on; soon one by one the family will come in from the fields, and the old woman now hastens to prepare the simple meal. A joint of smoked mutton, taken from the racks overhead, is laid on the hot cinders, and by the time the family have assembled it is roasted. This joint is sometimes varied with salted fish or a pilau. Very commonly, however, flesh and fish are alike wanting, and only vegetables appear upon the table. However, all are content. The maidens come home from the fields, where they have been employed in digging or in hoeing, or engaged in tending the sheep or

---

* In some cottages an hour-glass is found, but this is not of frequent occurrence.

cattle on the upland pasture. The sons stroll in armed to the teeth with pistols and rifles, as though from a foray in Albania. Their occupation, however, has been more peaceful than their appearance indicates, they having just returned from the market at Cattaro, where they have been selling garden-stuff, the produce of the ground round the cottage, and the poultry which was roosting last evening in the midst of the family.

Every one, as he or she enters the house, kisses with respect the hands of the old couple, and not until this necessary salutation is over do they begin any familiar conversation. They now all prepare for the evening meal. First the old grandfather eats, then the men of the family seated round a large block of wood which serves them for a table, and then the women and children take their meal.

After the meal the evening rest commences. All the family gather around the hearth. The men smoke, the women sow, knit, or attend to the wants of the children. Then turn by turn the men relate stories of personal adventure. As a matter of course they begin to speak of past battles. The old father has some story of the days of the great Vladika, and tells of the number of white plumes which he himself received in acknowledgment of the Turks which he had slain with his own hands. Then the younger ones tell of the days of Grahova and of their exploits under Mirko, and look forward with undisguised satisfaction to the call that Montenegro will send forth when danger next threatens their mountain homes.

After these warlike recollections, which are always listened to with profound interest, those who have been at the market in Cattaro tell the news which they had heard there, and especially of anything that is taking place in Western Europe which promises to have an influence upon their own destinies. In the course of the evening neighbour after neighbour drop in and join the friendly circle, and the *gusle* is then brought out,* and lays of the ancient days of Servia, of Bosnia, of Ivan Beg, of Milosh Obilic, and of the glories of the reign of Stephen Dushan,

* 'This instrument is remarkable from having only one string, which is stretched from a long rack, and a wooden body, covered with parchment; its general shape being like a guitar. It is played with a bow. The sound is very plaintive and monotonous, and is principally used as an accompaniment to the voice; the performer singing the glorious wars of Montenegrin and Servian heroes; of Tzerni George and Milosh Obrenovich; of Tzernoievich and Milosh Obilich, or of the far-famed Scanderbeg, under whom their ancestors fought against the Turks.'—WILKINSON, vol. i. p. 440.

are droned out from that monotonous but national lyre. And when enough of these have been recited, songs of domestic love, of the deeds of the Hayduks, or weird lays of the Vila of the mountains,* fill up the evening.

And thus night draws on, and the time for bed, or at least for sleep, arrives; the friends who have come from the neighbouring cottages disappear, and as they move homeward the chant of a prayer is heard, until lost in the distance. At length the family are alone, and the members of it cluster into a corner of the room where hangs a rude painting of the name-saint of the family with a lamp burning before it. The old father then recites aloud a short prayer, which ends with the ancient form of the Orthodox Church, in which our Lord is asked to accord one and all 'a peaceful rest and safety from all evil angels.' And now, the day-duties at an end, the fire is covered up with ashes, and the mattresses are stretched out upon the floor of the cottage, and, wrapped in their strookas—but not before they have again kissed the hand of the house-elder and received his blessing—the different members seek their allotted places with their feet turned towards

* The Banshee, wraith, fairy, or protecting genius of the Serb people.

the fire, and without dreaming of fastening the door, in patriarchial simplicity they drop asleep, free from thought of danger because consciously under the protection of their God.*

* LENORMANT, *Turcs et Monténégrins.*

CHAPTER VIII.

MORAL CHARACTERISTICS — POSITION OF WOMEN — HONESTY—CHASTITY—COURT OF APPEAL—CODE OF LAWS—EQUALITY OF PEOPLE.

It is not to be supposed that the situation and poverty of the Montenegrins, and the life of unceasing warfare, or readiness for warfare, which their position forces upon them, can be unattended with evils which affect the character of these mountaineers, though it may be questioned whether these evils and disadvantages are not more than counterbalanced by much of solid gain, and the growth of virtues which are frequently lost sight of in more civilised communities. The life of the women is one of hard toil. They have to bear more of the material burdens of daily existence than the men, to the loss of their beauty. Their life is one of humiliation, perhaps of inferiority, though not, as in the Turkish provinces, of degradation. They are the companions, not the toys and slaves, of man, even though they may get more than their fair share of the duties which such companionship entails.

The need of constant watchfulness against the enemy on their frontiers has, it is said, produced a habit of craft in all classes in Montenegro; which is probably true, since this is almost always the result of a similar condition of the kind of warfare which they have to endure. And though their practice of ready obedience to their Prince has put an end, within the borders of the Principality, to the vendetta, which was formerly resorted to, the Montenegrins, when at a distance from their own homes, and away from the control of their ruler, are said to be treacherous and implacable. They are, moreover, inclined to be vain of their personal prowess, and have an inordinate thirst for admiration. In matters of personal cleanliness there is much to be desired. It is the testimony of an admirer that 'Cetinje supplies everything but a tub,' but then he adds, 'a wise traveller carries that with him.'*
As to the people, water is scarce in their country, and is seldom resorted to for ablutions. Their linen is worn without change until it almost falls to pieces; add to this, they possess a fondness for

* FREEMAN.

spirituous liquors as great almost as their brethren and sisters in England.

All the vices attributed to the people of Montenegro, even if we grant their existence to the full, are, however, blended with great virtues. Their loyalty and patriotism are unimpeachable. Their courage, both active and passive, is undoubted. Though they are possessed with a reckless disregard of life when their country is endangered, suicide is seldom heard of among them; such an act being justly contemned as a proof of moral cowardice unworthy of a Montenegrin.* Their honesty is remarkable; crime is rare in Montenegro, and the respect paid by the men to females, not only to those of their own race, but also to those of their enemies, is generally acknowledged. Hence injuries to women and children are seldom if ever heard of in their inroads upon Turkey; † and the chastity of

* *Le Monténégrin Contemporain*, p. 393.

† 'Whatever their degradation may be, they possess broad distinctive marks of superiority over their Mussulman neighbours. One example of this is apparent in their heroic struggles against an overwhelming force for freedom. Another is the difference of their treatment of the weaker sex. Besides which the Turk is under superstitious influences from which the wildest Montenegrin is free, and labours under a savage fanaticism which presents, so long as it lasts, a hopeless bar to all progress.'—WINGFIELD, *Tour in Dalmatia and Montenegro*, p. 209.

both sexes is witnessed to by all who have written of the Montenegrin people, even by those not disposed to regard the Serb character too favourably. After speaking of their social customs, Lady Strangford says:—

'They have another virtue beside this simplicity of life; this is their perfect honesty. I happened to mention that I dropped a gold bracelet in Albania. "Had you dropped it here, even in the remotest corner of the Black Mountains, it would have been brought to me in three days," said the Prince. I am sure this was not mere talk, for I heard it confirmed by enemies as well as friends of the Montenegrins. I was frequently told of a traveller who left his tent, with the door open, on a Montenegrin hillside, and returned after three years' absence to find every single thing as he had left it. It is the old story of the devotion of a simple-minded people, and the just administration of a Homeric chieftain—all the more easily carried out in such a country as the Tzrnagora, because the Prince can be acquainted with the people as individuals, and can set them a personal example eagerly caught up by each of his loving subjects.'*

Be the reasons what they may, I add my testi-

---

* *Eastern Shores of the Adriatic*, p. 159.

mony to the rigid honesty of the Montenegrin people.* One use which is made of the little plane-tree in the centre of Cetinje is a deposit for found goods. Travellers in this country are as yet few, and the simple peasant, perhaps for that reason, is unperverted by contact with what is called 'civilisation.' Now if one chanced to drop an article on the road, and it was found by any one in Montenegro, the person who had lost the property might reckon on finding it laid at the root of the tree, or dangling from its branches, to be reclaimed by its owner. Few crimes, indeed, blacken the simple annals of these highlanders, and, save for border feuds and forays, now, however, rare, there would occur nothing to disturb the quiet of the Black Mountains save actual hostilities with the Turks or the expectation of approaching invasion. During the first five years of the reign of the present Prince, three executions occurred within the Principality, and when it is borne in mind that Prince Nicholas succeeded to power after the assassination of his predecessor at Cattaro; that vendetta had always been the practice, but had only two

* A writer not disposed to do full justice to these people, yet observes, ' I have not a word to say against the personal honesty of the Montenegrins.'—WINGFIELD, *A Tour in Dalmatia and Montenegro*, 1853, p. 184.

or three years before been made punishable by death; and that recent legislation had placed the murder of a Turk on the same footing as that of a Christian; and this in the teeth of inveterate practice and of old and even honoured tradition not soon nor easily forgotten—the criminal business of the Principality must be acknowledged light. This state of absolute security along the frontiers has not, indeed, been attained without the employment of a vigorous hand and the exercise of a determined will. During one of the progresses of the Vladika Peter II. (1830—1851), he is recorded to have left as many as fifteen culprits for execution. This, however, is a state of things which has wholly passed away.

In all that effects the position of woman and in the laws concerning personal purity, the principles of equity, which in communities boasting of a greater advance to civilisation are too frequently disregarded, have not been lost sight of by Montenegrin legislators. On this subject I cite the testimony of competent and unprejudiced witnesses.

'According to Danilo's code, the Montenegrin woman has, in every respect, the same legal rights as a man, and especial provision is made to secure her a full share in the division of property. When a father's possessions are parted among his children, daughters inherit as well as sons, and an only daughter can succeed to the whole property of both her parents. When a woman marries, she receives a dowry which passes to her husband's family, but in return, should she be left a widow, she is entitled to her husband's share in the common stock, and, should she marry again, the family of her first husband must continue her a certain pension. In cases of domestic quarrel, where a man refuses to dwell with his wife, they are at liberty to separate, but not to break the marriage. Neither of them may wed any one else, and the maintenance of the wife must be provided for by the husband. Further, care is taken by law that no woman be married against her inclination. When, as is usual, persons have been affianced in childhood, the priest is forbidden to marry them without having ascertained that the bride is a willing party; and if a girl should dislike the spouse chosen for her by her parents, and choose one for herself, the family is not allowed to interfere. 'Such couples,' so runs the sentence, 'are united by love.'

'A woman who murders her husband shall be put to death like any other murderer, only no weapon may be employed in her execution, for it is shameful to use arms against one who cannot take arms in defence.' By what agency a woman shall be executed is not provided by the code Danilo, but, according to ancient usage, in cases of gross crime she is stoned, her father casting the first stone. With this fearful doom was visited every transgression of social purity, and though Danilo's code sanctions capital punishment only in the case of a married woman, by popular custom there is no exception. Nor, according to Montenegrin standard, is the crime less degrading to the stronger than to the weaker culprit; the male offender equally forfeits his life, the honour of his family receives as deep a stain; while her father undertakes the punishment of the girl, the man is shot by his own relatives. Thus have they 'put the evil away from among them;' the Montenegrin spurns social impurity as unworthy of his manhood,* and even when dealing with their Mahommedan enemies, even in their wildest tchétas, with these 'barbarians' a woman is safe.

'It has been remarked that the social virtue of

* 'I asked the Prince what would be done to a woman who was unfaithful to her husband. He looked surprised, and said simply, 'They never are; if they had been, in former days they would have been put to death: I should confine them for life."—*The Eastern Shores of the Adriatic*, p. 156.

the Montenegrin is not less admirable in itself than as an evidence of what the precepts of Christianity can do for the moral life of a people even when its material life has been reduced to the verge of barbarism.' *

The respect evinced for women shows itself in a remarkable way. The protection of a woman gives to a criminal or to an enemy the most perfect immunity from danger. No one would venture to seize or attack any man to whom a woman had extended the sanctuary of her presence; so that in the most dangerous times, amid the conflict of war, her companion, however obnoxious he may be, either from private or public causes, is safe from the slightest molestation at the hand of a Montenegrin.†

Though the poverty of the Montenegrin people

* *Travels in Slavonic Provinces of Turkey*, vol. ii. pp. 267, 268, 2nd edition.

† 'A ce point de vue les mœurs des Tsernogortses sont entièrement chevaleresques. La femme est pour eux un être inviolable. Les vengeances, les querelles de tribus ou de familles ne l'atteignent pas. Elle jouit même du plus noble privilége. L'homme qu'une femme a pris sous sa sauvegarde, cût-il commis un meurtre, fût-il sous le coup de la plus implacable vendetta, devient aussi sacré qu'elle ; il peut avec elle venir s'asseoir au foyer de ses ennemis, nul n'oserait toucher à un cheveu de sa tête, car ce serait se déshonorer à jamais aux yeux de toute la nation.'—LENORMANT, p. 21.

stands greatly in the way of an extended hospitality to travellers, what they have is freely offered, and there is no country in Europe in which the safety of a visitor is regarded so greatly, and where his protection is deemed so much a point of national honour, as among these rugged mountains. In the times even of the greatest commotion the traveller in this country, wherever he may be, is absolutely safe.*

Such petty disputes as arise among so primitive a people are settled by the judges of the village or the *sirdar* of the district. The senators are the chief judges of all matters which arise within their own districts, and the assembled Senate is the ultimate court of appeal from that of the *palica* or district. In more intricate or difficult disputes the decision of the Senate is given by the mouth of the President. The Prince, however, is commonly appealed to to settle disputes, and his decision is sought not only by his own subjects but by the inhabitants of the Herzegovina, which, though once a part of Montenegro, has been for a long time in the possession of the Turks. 'Every peasant in the land, however poor,' says Lady Strangford, 'has a right to come to the Prince himself for judgment;

* Cyprien Robert, *Les Sclavs de Turquie.*

and such is their affection for him that no one would dream of questioning his justice. If the justice of his sentence is not evident to them, they say, 'He has a reason for it,' and acquiesce quietly. They are satisfied with the decisions of the Senate only as believing them to come from the Prince himself.'* A more recent traveller thus describes the court of justice at Cetinje:—

'In speaking of the metropolis of Montenegro I must not pass over unnoticed the senate-house and the senators of the Principality. Although for the trial of offenders charged with great crimes the senators meet within doors and have the assistance of a secretary to make a record of the cause, yet in ordinary cases this is not resorted to. The senate-house is, as the Prince's secretary jocosely remarked to me, the largest in Europe, and indeed in the world. All ordinary assemblies, whether for counsel or for the trial of civil and criminal causes, are held under the plane-tree in front of the palace, the heavens its roof and the horizon its boundaries, if indeed it has any. The Sunday evening after my arrival I strolled out of my lodgings about six o'clock, and found a court of justice then sitting.

* *Eastern Shores of the Adriatic*, pp. 157, 158.

The Prince was seated on a low wooden stool under the shade of the tree, whilst around him were ranged all the senators who happened to be in Cetinje. A few attendants with their rifles stood outside the circle of the senators, intermingled with a group of listeners, amongst the most interested of whom I may reckon myself. In the middle of the circle stood the plaintiff and defendant. The case was a disputed debt of a few piastres. Both spoke at once, and their pleadings were racy enough to elicit a joke or two from the Prince and laughter from the spectators. In the midst of the examination of the two parties to the suit—the only witnesses who appeared on this occasion—the horses were brought out for the use of the Prince in his customary afternoon's ride. Thereupon he soon summed up and gave judgment, apparently to the satisfaction of both parties, though evidently more to the satisfaction of one than of the other; since, though both came forward and kissed his hand, the successful suitor kissed the hem of his coat also. It was a very patriarchal scene, and such, I suppose, as might have been witnessed in the Highlands of Scotland little more than a century ago. The Prince told me afterwards that only trifling causes were thus disposed of, such in fact as required not so much the discrimination of 'a judge as the intervention of an arbitrator.' *

If the court of appeal is of this primitive character, the simplicity which reigns throughout the ordinary courts of justice would astonish men accustomed to the more artificial systems of Western Europe. No lawyer is reared on the soil of Montenegro. The judges, chosen by the people† yearly, on the Feast of St. Basil,‡ have no stated periods for their assize. The occurrence of a fair or a market, since it brings together a large number of people, is selected for the time of the gaol delivery of the district. Before this tribunal, seated always in the open air, plaintiff and defendant make their appearance, together with any witnesses they may deem necessary. The principals, having spoken in turn, and the witnesses having been heard, withdraw, and the judges discuss the merits of the case with the spectators, and consider the judgment they are about to give by the aid of the light which any one present may throw upon the matter in dispute. Having arrived at a conclusion, they then recall the plaintiff and defendant, and pronounce sentence, which is thereupon registered. Nothing else, how-

* *Good Words*, February, 1866.
† Code Danilo, art. 13. ‡ UBICINI.

ever, is written. There are no records of the pleadings and therefore no precedents; and, beyond a few brief paragraphs in the code of Prince Danilo, no statutes and no rules to guide the judge. Equity, common sense, the immutable laws of morality, and the acknowledged principles of Montenegrin justice alone regulate the proceedings. As there are no special advocates, should either of the principals in the suit be not gifted with sufficient eloquence to plead his own cause—a circumstance, however, which rarely happens—one of the auditors is always ready to lend his aid and to enact the part of an advocate.*

The principles of equity, which are common to all people, the traditionary laws of the old Serbian monarchy, and especially some precepts attributed to Stephen Dushan, made up until almost our own time the common law of Montenegro, and this unwritten code was for a long time the only law known throughout the Principality. At the close of the last century, however, Peter I. issued a code of laws consisting of thirty-three articles. These were republished with additions in 1855 by Prince Danilo, extending the code to ninety-three articles.

A few of these articles will give the reader some

* LENORMANT.

idea of the spirit of the laws which regulate the lives and actions of the Montenegrin people.* The code contains simple laws to restrain murder, acts of violence, the *vendetta* formerly practised, and robbery. It provides for the appointment of judges and defines their qualifications, and prescribes the punishment for unjust judgment. Since judges are chosen by the people, one of the articles of the code declares it to be their duty to fulfil the obligations imposed upon them by this choice, and to labour to maintain peace among their fellow-countrymen. For this end the judges are forbidden to engage in traffic or to travel out of their own country.† On taking their seat for the trial of any cause they are to remember: 1. That by the voice of God and the will of the people they have been chosen judges, the fathers and lovers of their country. 2. They are to pray God to enlighten their minds and to give them

---

* This code was printed under the title of 'Zakonek.— Daniela Prvog Knesa e Gospodara Slobodne Chrnegore e Brdah.—1855." An official translation into Italian, "Codice di Danilo, Primo Principe e Signore del Libero Montenero e della Perda," was at the same time printed. The code occurs also in a French translation, in the volume of MON. DELARUE, *Le Monténégro* (Paris, 1862), and, together with the code of Peter I., in MON. LENORMANT's book, *Turcs et Monténégrins* (Paris, 1866).

† Art. 13, Code Danilo.

intelligence to discern the right and the wrong of the matter before them.* 3. They are to remember their oaths to act impartially and to decide with equity without regard to the position of either party in the suit. 4. They are to hear each party, and not to allow both to speak at the same time, but they are to require them to speak without passion and slowly, so that the clerk may take notes of their evidence, and the judges may understand the grounds of their complaint or defence.† Should a judge ask or receive a gift, he is at once to be degraded from his office. The judge who insults either party in a suit is to pay a fine to the Treasury, whilst an insult offered to a judge is punished by a like fine, and the imprisonment of the guilty party. Theft of cattle —oxen or horses—belonging to natives of Montenegro or the Berda, whether living there or in Austrian territory, is, according to the Code of Peter I., to be punished as murder, and that because 'he who steals the ox or horse of another causes more sorrow and tears to the whole family than if he had killed one of its members, especially if the owner be poor, and has no other ox or horse, for then being unable to buy another he would be

---

* Art. 22, Code Peter I.
† Art. 22, Code Peter I.; Art. 6, Code Danilo.

compelled to sell his land or other goods in order to buy those animals, without which he could not live.'* It is to be noted that whilst the code of Peter I. only makes it an offence to steal cattle from Montenegrins, either within the territory of the Prince, or from those living in Herzegovina, Albania, Dalmatia, and other Austrian states, the code of Danilo has extended the prohibition to the whole of the border, whether Turkish or Austrian.†

If a man wishes to sell his real property—his house, fields, vineyard, or forest ground—he must first offer it in the presence of witnesses to his relatives; if these are unwilling to purchase, he must then offer it to his nearest neighbours, and only on their refusal can he put it up to public sale; the relatives or the neighbours are, however, not to take advantage of this law to the detriment of the seller. If they purchase they are to do so at the same price which others are willing to give, since it is to be offered at a fixed valuation.‡ As markets are instituted for the good of the people, no one must

---

* Art. 17, Code Peter I.; Arts. 24 and 25, Code Danilo.

† 'Qualunque trasgressione commessa da un Montenegrino o Berdiano in uno stato contermino andrà soggetta alla pena, da cui sarebbe colpita se avvenuta nell' interno.'—*Cod. Danilo*, art. 25.

‡ Art. 45 and 46, Code Danilo.

disturb the peace at such places 'any more than they would quarrel in a church,' and those who commence or excite disturbances in either market or church are to be similarly punished.* Injury to the person is assessed according to the members injured, and the aggressor is required in addition to pay all costs incurred in the cure of the wounded man.† A blow by hand, foot, or pipe may be avenged by killing the aggressor; but if the injured person allows a day or two to elapse and then kills his opponent, he is guilty of murder. All brigandage on the Turkish frontier is forbidden in time of peace or during a truce, and in case of breach of this law the booty is to be restored and the criminal punished.‡ The son or daughter who treats either parent with disrespect is for the first offence to be fined, for the second to be imprisoned and flogged, for the third the father is at liberty to turn the offender out of the house and to deprive him or her of all the rights of a child.§

That these laws may be observed throughout Montenegro, it is enjoined not only upon all priests, but also upon the chiefs of each district, in church

---

* Art. 19, Code Peter I.; Art. 83, Code Danilo.
† Art. 33, Code Danilo.   ‡ Art. 26, Code Danilo.
§ Art. 58, Code Danilo.

on all holy days, to call upon all the heads of families to live in peace and brotherhood one with another, to fear God, to abstain from evil deeds and evil speaking, and to obey the laws, for, as this document very sensibly goes on to say, 'since the law is made in order to prevent crime, it is necessary that it should be known by every one, so that none may plead ignorance in excuse for breaking it.' * By the last article of the code of Peter I. it is declared to be the duty of every Montenegrin to be faithful to his country, from which no prosperity should separate him, as nothing should induce him to change his religion or betray or in any way be unfaithful to his brethren or his nation; for the lawgiver goes on to say 'we are all bound to these conditions, since we are born and have been brought up in one and the same country.' †

In 1871 the attention of the present Prince was directed to the improvement of the code of his predecessor, and a commission was formed for the purpose of drawing up a new code of laws. Little progress had been made in this when the urgent need of attending to the reform of the military organization, and then first the prospects of war, and afterwards actual warfare, prevented the

* Art. 32, Code Peter I.　　† Art. 33, Code Peter I.

intentions of the Prince from being carried into effect. The Montenegrins are still controlled and regulated by the patriarchal institutes of Peter I. and Danilo, of which I have given some specimens.

Until recent times the most treasured trophy of a Montenegrin was the head or heads of the Turks whom he had slain in battle; a row of these ghastly tokens of victory used formerly to decorate the tower which rises behind the monastery in Cetinje, the residence of the Vladika who ruled over the Principality, in the same way that only a few years before Temple Bar in London was adorned with the heads of Tory gentlemen who preferred the House of Stuart to that of Hanover. These heads have disappeared from Cetinje for more than twenty years, and it is now denounced as a crime, punishable by imprisonment, for a Montenegrin to carry off the head of his enemy from the field of battle. It is a great testimony to the deference paid to the commands of these Princes that the last three rulers have succeeded in repressing this savage practice. Two years ago, among the few criminals suffering imprisonment, was one whose crime was that he had brought away the head of a Turk slain at Podgoritza. At present the ramparts of the tower on which these trophies of war were once placed is occupied with beehives.

The first article of the code of Prince Danilo recites the fact that all the inhabitants of Montenegro and of the Berda are equal in the eyes of the law;* all are regarded as noble; all possess property in land; all are eligible for the few offices which exist in the Principality; there is no standing army, whilst all bear arms, and almost all are skilled in their use. Where these conditions exist, it matters little what the form of government is: the result must needs be a free constitution. The technical terms of Western constitutional law are hardly applicable to either Montenegro or Serbia. In both countries we have the full tide of democratic liberty controlled and regulated by that idea which lies at the root of all Slavonic institutions—the sacredness and strength of the family tie.† To the

---

* 'Ogni Montenerino e Berdiano è equale in faccia alla legge.'

† 'Sur aucun point du globe, l'égalité n'existe peut-être aussi complète que dans le Tsernegore; mais le principe d'égalité, tel qu'il est compris et pratiqué par les Slavos, ne menace point les droits et l'existence de la famille, comme les théories qu'on fait reposer en France sur ce même principe. Chaque Serbe, en jouissant de son indépendance, continue d'être dévoué aux intérêts de tous; il ne se sépare presque jamais de ses parents.'—CYPRIEN ROBERT, t. i. p. 104.

Montenegrin the Prince is the father of the country and of every individual within its limits; his orders are obeyed as dutiful children obey the commands of a father whom they love and honour; his wish is law, as the wishes of a parent are regarded and esteemed by dutiful children, whilst he, on his part, is bound to regard not only the interests of his subjects, but also their wishes.

CHAPTER IX.

OCCUPATIONS—LAND TENURE—OFFICES—INCOME—EXPENDITURE.

THE Montenegrins are a nation of agriculturists, herdsmen, and shepherds. This may have arisen from choice; it is imposed upon them by necessity. Cut off from the coast, they are unable to employ their energies in commerce, and their poverty prevents them, as a general rule, from employing or even requiring the aid of skilled artizans. Each family manufactures the coarse cloths and linen required for its own use, and the simple garments, sandals, and shoes which they wear are of home workmanship. The arms which they carry, and which are inseparable from the Montenegrin, were until recently manufactured at Prisrend, at Ipek, at Travnik, or at Seraievo, in Bosnia and in Albania. Now, however, the arsenal and armoury near Rjeka, where rifles and pistols can be made, or old ones repaired and adapted to modern requirements, renders them in a great measure independent of foreign supplies. The masonry and carpenters' work required in the construction of their houses does not call for specific workmen, and if greater skill is demanded than the peasants possess workmen are hired from Dalmatia and Serbia.* The ablest senator or the most trusted warrior employs himself like the Romans of old in the manual labour which his small patrimony demands, but the same legislator or soldier would consider it a degradation to be engaged in a trade or to labour at some profitable art. The possession of a seaport, so greatly desired, and surely not for ever to be withheld from them, will produce a change in this respect; but so long as the people of Montenegro are excluded from the coast, and are menaced by Turkey and their territory coveted by Austria, the labours of the field are alone possible or even desirable for them. The occupation of the peasant mountaineer is that which fits him best for the maintenance of his freedom, and prevents him from sinking to the

---

* 'There are few Montenegrins who exercise any trade; though some perform the offices of blacksmiths, farriers, or whatever else the immediate wants of a village may require.' —WILKINSON, vol. i. p. 430.

level of his brethren in the adjoining provinces of Turkey.

The land of Montenegro is divided into two classes, arable and grazing: the former possessed by individuals, or more usually by families; the latter is the common possession of the people of the whole district in which it is situated. There are no State domains in the Principality beyond some small property belonging to the two monasteries of Cetinje and Ostrog, and the largest landed proprietor is the holder of sixty acres. The other possessions range from freehold estates of two acres up to the modest dimensions of twenty acres. Although the arable lands are commonly held by a family, or, to use the significant Montenegrin phrase, 'by the house,' not by the individual, yet each member of a family has the right, after conference with the rest, to separate his own share from the family estate, and to sell or mortgage his possession to his relatives, and, on their refusal to purchase, then to sell it to any other person. No child, however, can claim a separate possession in land during the lifetime of the father.[*] Up to the present time the practice has been for the sons to reside with their parents, to cultivate the family land in common, so long as the father is

[*] Art. 47, Code Danilo.

living, and on his death to continue to till the soil and share the proceeds in partnership (*Zadrooga*) ; * though when the father is dead they may exercise the right of dividing their share from that of the rest. Accordingly, the primitive and patriarchal system of holding their lands in common has been of late years frequently departed from.

A Montenegrin thus explained this custom to me : 'With us the bad divide the land and live apart; the good keep the land undivided and live together.' Where this is accepted as an axiom, of course 'the good' predominate; and in houses of only two large rooms three generations, or even more, may often be found living together; brothers with their wives and large families dwelling harmoniously in the same apartment.

When lands are shared, each son has a right to an equal part, as well as of the movable property, and no distinction is made between the elder and the younger son, except as a matter of practice,

* For an account of the Zadrooga, as it exists in Free Serbia, see Appendix B to *Travels in South Slavonic Countries*, by MISSES MACKENZIE and IRBY, vol. ii. p. 329, 2nd edition, 1877. 'The Zadrooga is a sort of community of property, household, labour, and revenue, among the members of the same family living together, under a *staréshina*, or free-elected, well-qualified leader, most frequently the father or grandfather of all.'—YOVANOVITCH.

though not of right. The rifle, knife, and pistols of the father are given to the eldest son. If there are sons the married daughters have no share either in the landed or movable property of the family, each of them having received at her marriage a portion of linen, dresses, and personal ornaments.*
When a man, however, dies without sons, the daughters inherit his land and other possessions, with the exception of the house and the garden around it and also his arms, which become the property of his brothers or their sons. This is in the case of several daughters surviving. When there is only one daughter, she usually, with the consent of her relatives, brings as her dower the whole of her father's property, of whatever kind it may be.†

As to the grazing lands and woods, these are the property, not of individvals, but of the community or clan (*pleme*) which is settled on them. All houses or families belonging to this clan have equal right of pasturage for cattle on these lands, and an equal right also to cut what wood they may require. This common right and a common church are the only ties which unite the whole clan, as there are no municipalities, and the Prince is the only authority

---

* Art. 51, Code Danilo. † Arts. 53, 55, Code Danilo.

which binds together the whole country into one state. Formerly, indeed, except in time of war, there was no central authority to which the whole country could defer. The affairs of each *celo*, or village territory, were regulated by the *staréschina*, assisted by the heads of the various families assembled in council; that of the *pleme* by the *knez*, assisted by the assembly of the tribe or clan; whilst each *nahia* was directed by an *obor knez* and by the assembly or diet of the whole nahia. The chiefs formerly possessed these various offices by virtue of hereditary right. Now the persons who fill these offices are selected by the Prince, but yet with a certain deference to the expressed wish of the *celo*, *pleme*, or *nahia*.

In Montenegro every one is included in the *pleme* where he resides. In every *pleme*, clan, or district, inhabited by families having a common ancestor,* there is one *voyvoda* and one civil governor. The dignity of *voyvoda* and of civil governor, however, is sometimes united in the same person; but more commonly the *voyvoda* is of one family, and the governor of another. The *voyvoda* is the military leader of the *pleme*. His office was hereditary, and descended from the father to the

* 'Plémens ou grandes familles.'—DELARUE.

eldest son. When a *voyvoda* died without sons, this dignity passed to the brother, nephew, or cousin who was the oldest male in the family, and remained in his hands until a like failure of direct descendants took place. Every *pleme* has, in addition to the *voyvoda*, a deputy (*serdar*), a dignity, like that of the *voyvoda*, formerly hereditary, but latterly it has been conferred by the Prince according to his pleasure; a change necessitated indeed by the new military organization of the nation. The administration of justice and the civil government of the *pleme* is usually entrusted to one who, though chosen by the Prince, has been marked out for the office by the confidence of the clan to which he belongs, and this consequently, like that of *voyvoda*, is not now an hereditary office. These two, the military leader and the civil governor of each nahia, assemble at Cetinje and compose the Senate of fourteen—or, with the president and vice-president, sixteen—members, the standing council of the Prince. Five of these senators reside wholly at Cetinje, the remaining nine are only in residence for three months in the year, in lodgings provided for them at the public expense, and receive, as an *honorarium* rather than a stipend, the first class of five a sum of £60, the latter class only £30, of

English money yearly. The President of the Senate, who holds rank next to the Prince, and is the most considerable of his civil subjects, receives an annual income of about £140, and the Vice-President about £120; the secretary of the Prince, who is also 'clerk of parliament' to the Senate, receives about £100 of English money.* These senators, like the Conscript Fathers of the old Roman Republic, are not only the leaders in war, but they also guide the plough, or more frequently handle the spade and reap the harvests of their paternal fields.†

The income and expenditure of the Government of Montenegro are arranged on a most economical scale. The most considerable item in the receipts consists of an annual sum of 10,000 sequins, or almost 47,000 florins, paid by Russia as an idemnity for losses in the days of Peter the Great, and in acknowledgment of services rendered by Montenegro in the war of the French Revolution. To this has of late years been added an annual gift from France of 50,000 francs.‡ Whether, however, this latter

---

* Until the last five or six years this *honorarium* was about two-thirds of the present amount.

† 'Comme le reste de ses concitoyens, le sénateur monténégrin se fait lui-même sa chaussure et les harnais de son mulet.'—LENORMANT.

‡ UBICINI.

sum is still paid I am unable to say. The family or house tax brings into the treasury about 35,000 florins. *Ad valorem* duties of four per cent. on articles exported and imported produce about 25,000 florins. A tax of one *zwanzig*, or twenty kreutzers (4*d*.), on every plough land (*kalo*), that is as much land as an ox can plough in one day;* five kreutzers on each hive of bees, and the same sum on every pig; three on each vine; two on every sheep; ten on every cow, ox, or other beast of burden; together with the *appalto* of tobacco; a tithe of the fishery on the Rjeka; and the rent of certain convent lands let to peasants—make up a sum reaching to about 220,000 florins, or £25,000 English money. These taxes, with the exception of course of the *ad valorem* duty on goods imported, are levied in October and January of each year, and for the payment of these the captain of each district is responsible. The customs duties are collected at Niegush, Rjeka, and Grahova. In times of war no taxes are levied.

In 1868 the civil list of the Prince was fixed at 6,000 Austrian ducats, or about £2,820 of English money. This sum, however, was charged with the

* This tax was formerly two zwanzigs, but it has been recently reduced one-half.

payment of some of the state officials. The next year, however, the Prince was released from these payments, and since 1869 he enjoys this civil list without abatement.*

The chief items of expenditure are the palace expenses, which are extremely moderate; the cost of maintaining the printing-office, established by Peter II.; gratuities to the Prince's guards, each of whom receives 60 thalers yearly; payments to the senators, and compensation money for expenses incurred by the captains and by the small body of artillerymen who compose the nucleus of the army, and salaries to the masters of the schools established by the present Prince and his two immediate predecessors. Add to this, in times of want—and times of want are not infrequent in those sterile domains —the purse of the Prince is the common fund to which all feel a right to resort. For what is the Prince but the father of the country? and to whom have children, when in need, a better right to apply than to their father?

* *Le Monténégro Contemporain*, p. 352.

CHAPTER X.

LANGUAGE—LITERATURE—PRINTING PRESS.

The Montenegrins are Serbs, consisting in part of the descendants of the old inhabitants of the Principality, in part of Serb refugees from Serbia, the Herzegovina, and Bosnia, who, at the time of the conquest of these provinces by the Turks, or subsequently, fled from their homes and found shelter within the natural defences of this rugged territory. At that time Montenegro, with the shores of the Bocche di Cattaro, formed the western verge of the empire of Stephen Dushan and of Lazar, who was defeated and slain at Kossova. It cannot be doubted that when these provinces of the Eastern Roman Empire were conquered and first tenanted by the Slavs, several of the old colonists—whether of Greek or Roman race—remained in their old possessions and became assimilated to the conquerors. To this cause writers on Montenegro have attributed the classical features, unlike the Slav type of countenance which are to be found in various parts of the present Principality.*

The language spoken throughout Montenegro is the Serbian dialect of the Slavonic. As the Serbian language itself has been spoken of as Italianized Slavonic,† so the Serbian of Montenegro—though probably the purest existing form of this language—has been enriched beyond that of Serbia with a number of Italian words, as well as with several from the Turkish. Original, scientific, and historical treatises are as yet infrequent in Serbian; but its capabilities to give expression to the language of fancy and of passion has been shown in the collections of poems, which form a considerable item in Serbian literature. It is believed to approach nearer than any other of the Slav dialects to the

---

* 'Le Serbe, émigrant au quatorzième siècle au Monténégro, y trouva les descendants de la race primitive auxquels Grecs et Romains s'étaient déjà successivement mêlés; plus tard le contact des Turcs, des Bosniaques et des Albanais apporta nécessairement son contingent d'influence, et enfin d'assez nombreuses familles, telles que la famille régnante actuelle, proscrites ou fuyant le commerce des Ottomans ou leur persécutions, vinrent des pays voisins chercher un refuge dans la Montagne-Noire.'—*Le Monténégro Contemporain*, p. 127.

† SCHLEGEL.

original or old Slavonic language, into which the Scriptures were translated in the ninth century by Cyril and Methodius, the apostles of the Slav lands. The language which they fixed by their translation of the Scriptures into it remains the ecclesiastical language of all the Orthodox Christians of the various Slav countries to the present day.

The Serbian language is at the present day spoken, with modifications, from the Black Sea to the Adriatic. A Montenegrin in Russia, Dalmatia, Croatia, or Serbia understands the speech of these several countries, and is in turn perfectly understood by these people when using his own tongue. Even in Bulgaria he has little difficulty in making himself understood. The Serbs, however, who have embraced the Roman Catholic faith, have, with many other national traits, laid aside the Cyrillic letters in use among their Orthodox brethren, and have long employed the Latin alphabet.

Although comparatively few treatises on history have been written in modern Serbian, the history of Montenegro has been transmitted in the ballads and poems which constitute the larger portion of its literature, and which, being independent of the printing-press, and having been preserved by popular recitations, have done much to keep alive the intellectual vigour of these peoples. These songs are stored up in the memory of the whole people, and are the delight alike of youth and old age, of prince and of peasant. The poems which celebrate the actions of the heroes of Serbia in the national struggle to arrest the armies of the Ottoman invaders have been compared to the cycle of Arthurian romances, in which the exploits of the heroes of the Round Table have been preserved and embodied in the literature of Europe. Allowing for the strictly historical character of the incidents celebrated in the Serbian songs, and the large, or as some assert the exclusively, mythological elements of the English poems, the comparison is not an inapt one.* The heroes of the cycle are King Lazar, Milosh, Strachimir Ivo, or Ivan-Beg, George Brankovic, and those other warriors who for a time upheld the falling fortunes of the Serbian race. In these songs enthusiastic travellers have seen, or imagined that they saw, the materials for a new Iliad and Eneid, which only await the hand of genius to be added to the great poems which are the common heritage of the world.†

* *Les Slaves de Turquie*, par CYPRIEN ROBERT, t. i. p. 124.
† CYPRIEN ROBERT, t. i. p. 125.

Specimens of these Serbian poems were made familiar to English readers of a past generation by means of a small volume of translations published by the late Sir John Bowring,* and to the present generation by a volume of paraphrases rather than translations printed by the present Lord Lytton (Owen Meredith).† Most travellers and writers on Montenegro have given selections, abstracts, and literal translations of several of these songs. It is true that these translations have for the most part been derived from French or German sources, and therefore can hardly be depended upon for minute accuracy, yet they are sufficiently close to the original to allow of a general idea being formed of the usual character of the popular songs of Serbia and Montenegro.

The vein of poetry, to which we are indebted for the old records of these mountaineers, is by no means exhausted amongst the Montenegrins of the present day. The present Prince has added to the literary stores of his country by the publication of a tragedy as well as by a volume of songs, which

---

* *Servian Popular Poetry.* Translated by JOHN BOWRING. 1827.

† *Serbski Pesme: or, National Songs of Servia*, by OWEN MEREDITH. 1861.

are popular throughout the Principality. The late Grand Voivode Mirko, the fiery paladin of Montenegro, the commander-in-chief of the people in the late war, the President of the Senate, the father and first subject of Prince Nicholas, was the author of a volume of poems which has reached a second edition.* The gift of song seems indeed to be one of the hereditary possessions of the house of Petrovic of Niegush; and the last two Vladikas, the sainted Peter I. and Peter II., were both poets of no mean power. The pleasure which these songs afford to the whole people may in part arise from the interest felt by all for the stirring incidents celebrated by the Montenegrin lyre; but in part it is to be attributed to a fondness and a taste for literature in the abstract which has ever honourably distinguished these mountaineers.

The first books printed in the Slavonic language issued from the presses of Cetinje and Rjeka from types cast at Venice, by the direction of Prince George IV., who governed Montenegro from 1490 to 1497. Copies of church books printed at his expense are preserved in the library of Prince Nicholas at Cetinje, and in the public library at

---

* *Junacke Spomenek. od Velekoga Vojvode Merka Petrovic.* The second edition was printed at Cetinje in 1864.

Belgrade, and are of rare beauty.* The original printing-presses both at Rjeka and Cetinje having been destroyed during one or other of the numerous wars with Turkey, one was re-established by Peter, the second Vladika of that name, at Cetinje. The few books which I have seen printed at this press are of very creditable workmanship.

That at such an early period a fugitive people should have taken advantage of the new art is among the most creditable facts of their remarkable history. 'It was in 1484 that the printing-press was set up at Cetinje, in a petty principality; they who set it up were men worsted in war and flying for their lives. Again, it was only seven years after the earliest volume had been printed by Caxton in the rich and populous metropolis of England; and when there were no printing-presses in Oxford, or in Cambridge, or in Edinburgh. It was only sixteen years after the first printing-press had been established (1468) in Rome, the capital of Christendom; only twenty-eight years after the appearance (1456) of the earliest printed book, the first-born of the great discovery.'† This printing-press, however, was destroyed when the Turks occupied Cetinje for a short time. The present office, the Clarendon,

* See note at end of this chapter. † GLADSTONE.

or Pitt Press of the Principality, only dates from the days of Peter II. This Vladika re-established printing in Montenegro in 1832.

Whilst the constant state of warfare in which these people have been born, reared, and died have not permitted any leisure for the pursuit of literature, the destructive forays of the Turks have deprived them of such means as they required to keep alive the least vestiges of literary taste. What the Turks did not destroy was concealed by the Montenegrins to escape falling into their hands, and afterwards often forgotten until accidentally discovered at some distant time. An office-book, printed on vellum, and heavily covered with silver, which lay for many years thus hidden in a well, is still shown, damaged, dilapidated, but respected as a relic of the past literary glories of Montenegro. In the monastery at Ostrog a few old tattered books, the remains of the former library in the place, are still shown; but, with the exception of the private library of the Prince, no collection of books worthy of the name of a library is to be found in the whole of Montenegro.

The popular folk-lore and tales which circulate round the cottage hearth have been collected by Vuk Stephanovic, who has done much in the way of collecting and preserving the folk-lore, proverbs, and popular history of the different branches of the Serbian people. From his collection of popular tales and myths a selection was made and translated into German more than twenty years ago by Jacob Grimm.* In English some specimens of these popular tales may be seen in a volume translated by Madame Mijatovic; † and, under the auspices of Bishop Strossmayer, a collection of Serbo-Bosniac legends and folk-lore tales have been recently published in Croatia.

* *Volksmärchen der Serben.* Berlin, 1854.
† *Serbian Folk-lore.* London, W. Isbister and Co., 1874.

⁎ The learned keeper of the public library at Belgrade furnished me, when I was about to visit Montenegro, with the accompanying note on three of the earliest volumes which were printed in the Principality during the fifteenth century:—

1. The *Octoëchos*, or book of songs and hymns of the Church, from the writings of S. John Damascene, was printed by the Reverend Archimandrite Macarius at Cetinje, with the blessing of Vavila, or Babylas, Metropolitan of Zeta, in A.D. 1493. The book, which is in folio, is printed in Cyrillic type of a beauty which has never been surpassed by any book printed in after times. It contains 270 folios.

2. The *Psalter*, with the canons of the Blessed Virgin and the chief saints of the Church, together with the Hours and Matin and Vesper offices. Printed by command of Prince George Tzrnojevic, with the blessing of the Metropolitan

Vavila, by the Archimandrite (*per hyeromonachum*) Macarius, in Cetinje, in Montenegro, A.D. 1495, in 4to. This contains 348 folios, and is printed with the same type as the last-named book.

3. The *Enchologion*, to which is added a *Rituale*, printed at Cetinje, A.D. 1495, in 4to. It contains 256 folios, and is printed with the same type as both the last-named books.

CHAPTER XI.

ECCLESIASTICAL STATE—EDUCATION.

In ecclesiastical matters Montenegro is a portion of the Orthodox Eastern Church, and, with the exception of a few persons who have taken refuge in this country, and who for the most part live on the southern frontier, all the inhabitants are members of this Church. The Koutchi nahia, however, which has just reunited itself to Montenegro, is for the most part Roman Catholic, and there are several Serb Mussulmans living in the Berda, who enjoy perfect toleration in religious matters, and who join with their Christian brethren in the defence of their common country.* It is expressly declared

* 'La tolérance religieuse est si absolue dans la Principauté monténégrine, que certaines parties des Berdas sont habitées par des Mussulmans qui ont paisiblement leurs imans et leur mosquées. Malgré la différence des religions, ces Mussulmans sont les frères d'armes des Tsernogortses

by the Code of Prince Danilo that all strangers settled in Montenegro shall possess the same civil and religious rights as the natives of the Principality.*

The whole Principality, with the exception of the Koutchi, is governed in ecclesiastical matters by an archbishop—Hilarion Ragonovic—who, however, as is not unusual in the Eastern Church, has no suffragan bishop under him.† The full title of this prelate is 'Metropolitan of Scanderia and the seacoast, Archbishop of Cetinje, Exarch of the Holy Throne of Pek, and Vladika of Tzrnagora.' Much of this, however, is entirely titular. As Montenegro was at one time a province of the Western Empire, its people were then in communion with the see of Rome and under the jurisdiction of the Pope. The see of the Metropolitan of the old province of the Zeta was at first at Skodra.‡ It was then removed

---

chrétiens; ils combattent avec la même ardeur contre les Ottomans, et chez eux la passion de l'indépendance nationale remplace l'exaltation de la foi religieuse qui anime leurs compatriots.'—LENORMANT, Introd. p. lxxvi.

* "Strainero di qualsivoglia professione religiosa potrà vivervi tranquillamente e fruire della libertà e dei nostri diritti speciali goduti dai nativi del Montenero e della Berda."—*Cod. Danilo*, § 92.

† CODINUS, *Notitiæ Græcorum Episcopatuum*.

‡ LE QUIEN, *Oriens. Christ.*, ii. 275, 278.

to Dioclea, and in the ninth century had at least twelve bishops suffragans under it. In the same century Montenegro was included within the Patriarchate of Constantinople. Its possession was for many years a point of dispute between the Pope and the Œcumenical Patriarch, when finally it was acknowledged as a part of the Patriarchate of the East.

From the time of the independence of Montenegro, after the battle of Kossova, and until the flight of the Patriarch of Ipek in 1769, the Montenegrin prelate was under his jurisdiction, but from that date he has been independent of any superior, except in reference to the spiritual deference due to the Patriarch of Constantinople. His income reaches the modest amount of £250 yearly, derived from the rent of lands belonging to the monasteries of Cetinje and Ostrog. Next in rank to the Archbishop are the Archimandrites of these two monasteries: the only convents in Montenegro deserving this name. Scattered over the country there are indeed ten monasteries, several of great antiquity, but almost all these are inconsiderable as regards the number of their inmates. Throughout the whole of Montenegro, probably, there are not twenty monks, and several of the monasteries are ruled and served by one priest, who is at once hegemon and simple monk, the governor and the body governed.

The monasteries in Montenegro are—1, at Ostrog, including Upper Ostrog, a hermitage with a famous shrine, which is sometimes mentioned as a distinct monastery from that of the Lower Ostrog; 2, Cetinje; 3, Moratcha; 4, Bratcheli, a double monastery; 5, Dobrisko; 6, Sdrebanik; 7, Celija Piperska; 8, Dugas; 9, Vikenlina Celija, near Gablac; 10, Malinsko. The monasteries throughout Montenegro, I believe with hardly an exception, are merely parish churches served by unmarried priests. These priest-monks, in addition to the care of the people within a certain district or parish, undertake the education of one or more lads, who are at the same time their pupils and assistants. The utter decay of the old monastic spirit of these countries is evident both in Serbia and in Montenegro. This arises in part, it may be, from a disinclination of the people for the monastic life—a disinclination which will extinguish the last vestiges of monasticism in these countries before many years are over; in part it is due to the circumstances of the country, which demands the active powers of all its sons—a demand hardly compatible with the monastic state. The description of one of these monasteries will give a fair idea of most of these establishments:—

'The church and the half-a-dozen rooms which make up the monastery of Celija Piperska, are situated on a small plateau or mound overlooking the Turkish territory near Spush. It has only one monk, who has to enforce and obey his own rule. In a small apartment—a part of the belfry—however, I was introduced to an old bed-ridden monk, who has been blind for the last ten years, and has found an asylum at this place. Like everything else near the Turkish frontier, the outer walls of the monastery, the walls of the church within, and even the walls of all the apartments, are loopholed for defence. The church, as an inscription over the west door informs the visitor, was restored in 1848. In the choir is the coffin of a Montenegrin saint— one Stephen, who, flying from the persecutions of the Mahommedans in the Herzegovina, towards the end of the seventeenth century, lived a saintly life at this place. On his death the people living near his retreat built a church to perpetuate his memory, and canonized him, as it were, by acclamation. This is the case with most of the Montenegrin saints, whose names will not be found in any calendar save this popular one. The church is remarkable for a low stone synthronus* behind the altar, the only one which I saw in Montenegro.'

The parochial clergy are about four hundred and twenty in number. The churches, however, exceed the number of priests, and several, built as votive offerings, or within reach of a very few persons, are served by the same pastor. These churches are of one type, and are chiefly remarkable for their poverty. The services are of a very simple character. Though in most countries the fact that the parochial clergy work like the rest of the inhabitants with the spade and hoe, go armed with pistols and rifles, and are the captains of their parishioners in time of war, would prove injurious to their spiritual influence, even if it did not deteriorate their character, the Montenegrin priests, according to the testimony of most travellers, are respected by, and are deserving of the respect of, their flocks. A Montenegrin, if he should chance to meet one of these priests, is not content with lifting his hat to him; he places his hand on his breast, and taking with the other the hand of the priest, he lifts it to his lips. Whenever a priest enters a house he is saluted in the same

* *Synthronus*, a seat for the bishop and clergy behind the altar of a Greek church, and facing west.

respectful manner.* Poverty and their semi-military duties have, however, led to much neglect of ecclesiastical proprieties, and, except from his beard, and not always from that, it is often difficult to distinguish the priest from the lay people of his parish. This, however, is being remedied: the great ecclesiastical movement of our day has not been without influence even in these distant regions.

An effort has recently been made, though with but partial success, to found a seminary at Ostrog for the education of candidates for the ministry of the Church. The training for the priesthood is yet sadly deficient. Sermons are still rare; only in exceptional cases do any of the parochial clergy preach, and then only at Christmas and Eastertide. With the better education of the clergy, however, this exceptional condition of things will pass away. The cassock is being resumed by the parochial as well as by the monastic clergy; and the observances of the ecclesiastical state are more cared for than has at least been the case for many years. Baptism is now,

* 'J'aime à le dire, au Monténégro, comme partout où j'ai vécu, j'ai toujours vu la majeure partie des curés être les véritables imitateurs du Christ, les dépositaires fidèles de sa doctrine, et les dignes organes de la primaire instruction.'— VIALLA DE SOMMIÈRES, *Voyage Historique et Politique au Monténégro*, t. i. p. 367.

according to the custom in countries inhabited by the Greek race, at least occasionally administered by immersion. As yet, however, this is but of rare occurrence; the almost universal practice being that of trine aspersion.* A few years ago I was informed by Prince Nicholas that he believed his own child —he had then but one—was the only child within the bounds of Montenegro who had been baptized by immersion. Communicants, again, are rare,† and the sacrament of the Lord's Supper is scarcely ever received except on the eve of a journey, or, perhaps, at long intervals, on one of the greater feast days of the year.

It has been the practice to send a few young men destined to such official positions as require acquaintance with European ideas to Paris or St. Petersburg for their education. This, however, has been found to be attended with inconveniences which to some extent counterbalance the advantages of such education, and this, together with the general poverty of the Montenegrins, has prevented it being resorted to, except in a very few cases, and the people look forward with eagerness to the time when not only the simple but the higher and scientific education also may be received within their own

* Vialla, t. i. p. 101.   † Cyprien Robert, t. i. p. 103.

territory, and thus be wholly Montenegrin. This the great advance made in the general education of the people of Montenegro may render possible in a few years.

Until the time of the Vladika Peter II., the only semblance of instruction for children was that afforded by the monks or clergy, who received two or three youths to assist them in the cultivation of their fields, to wait upon them in their houses, and in the performance of their clerical duties; and who received in return just a sufficient amount of education to enable them to read the Church service. These servitors received ordination when of age, and became parish priests. Occasionally a Montenegrin youth, better educated in the schools of Serbia and Dalmatia, returned to his native country, and was ordained to the charge of a parish, or entered the ranks of the monastic clergy. This, however, was of infrequent occurrence, and the main body of the clergy had only such an imperfect education as they had been able to obtain whilst acting as servants in the small monasteries. As to the people, in the spirit of Goldsmith's Dutch Professor, they were content to know that they tilled their ground without book-learning, and could defend their country from the attacks of the Turks and fulfil the duties of soldiers and subjects of the Vladika without reading or writing.

Peter II. attempted to remedy this general lack of education, and during his rule, and by his care, two schools were instituted. One of these, however, disappeared in the subsequent war with Turkey.* His successor, Prince Danilo, not only revived these schools, but collected some young men of the chief families of Montenegro, and himself superintended their education within the walls of his palace at Cetinje. This example was not lost upon his people.† It stimulated them to corresponding exertions, and now the traveller, as he passes through the country, may see the youthful shepherd or goatherd sheltering himself from the rays of the noonday sun, under the shadow of a tree or of a rock, or at his cottage door when the day's work is at an

---

* 'It is owing entirely to the influence of the two last Vladikas that the Montenegrines have been raised from the level of mere savage defiant barbarism to the first stage of progressive civilisation. This civilisation is yet in its infancy; but from all I saw and heard, I venture to assert that the Montenegrines have all, from the Prince down to the poorest, awakened to a genuine desire for improvement.'— *The Eastern Shores of the Adriatic*, p. 143. That which was a desire in 1863 has brought forth good fruit since.

† *Le Monténégro Contemporain*, p. 363. *Turcs et Monténégrins*, Introd. p. lxxiv.

end, poring over a New Testament or a volume of Serbian poetry, or absorbed in the study of the songs which preserve with more fidelity than poetry the heroic history of their country.

At the death of Peter II., in 1851, the only school which existed in the whole Principality was an elementary one at Cetinje, established by him in 1832, and this only accommodated eighteen or twenty scholars, whose instruction was limited to reading and writing. A few years ago there were eight or ten boys' schools in Montenegro, and in 1868 a small seminary was established by Prince Nicholas at Cetinje, where youths destined for the ecclesiastical life, as parish priests or as schoolmasters, may be trained. The enlargement of the course of instruction has kept pace with the increase in the number of the schools. Within three years of the establishment of this seminary forty teachers were sent from it to conduct schools in various parts of Montenegro. The stipends assured to these teachers are fixed on a liberal scale, though the sum will appear small to us. They rise progressively until they reach about £24 a year. In addition to the stipend the teachers are provided with lodging and with firewood, contributed by the parents of the scholars.

At Cetinje, for several years past, some of the scholars have been maintained as boarders, in part at the expense of the Prince. The course of instruction, extending over four years, includes reading, writing, arithmetic, ecclesiastical music, the rudiments of geography, and sacred and profane history.* As to the national history, that is taught

* 'As to the school of Cetinje, our visit happened in the Christmas holidays, when regular lessons were not going on; but one afternoon, hearing from without the voices of children singing hymns, we entered and found scholars, but no teachers. It appeared that the boys of the first class were met to sing and read together. Their song was rough-voiced as that in a Scotch kirk; the books they had just laid down were church books; we were told that the Cyrillic translation of the Bible can be mastered with ease by a Montenegrin child. Reading, writing, arithmetic, history, and geography are taught at Cetinje; but the master not being present, there was no one to put the class through it individually. The boys showed their copy-books, in which the writing was very fair—of course in the Cyrillic character. Like the rest of the race, the Slaves of Montenegro show much eagerness for historical knowledge and quickness in picking up foreign languages. At present the poetic gift is common among them, and a poem on the death of the late Prince was produced by the Cetinje scholars. Schools were established by Danilo in many a village; but since his death the unsettled state of the surrounding country has gone much against their progress. In case of a Turkish inroad, the people know that their villages will be burnt and everything like civilisation put an end to; and in the meantime we heard of schoolmasters forsaking their desks for the more congenial post of volunteers in the Herzegovina. No

by the songs, which all have been long accustomed to learn, whether they could read or not.*

Practically, at the present time, education, though not compulsory, throughout Montenegro, since that would be alien to the independent spirit of the people, is yet universal. The desire for learning indeed is so great, that it is a common occurrence to find aged persons trying to learn to read. Until recently, however, though boys could receive their education in Montenegro without going any considerable distance from their own homes, there were no schools for girls in any part of the Principality. This, however, has been now remedied by Prince Nicholas, who has not only established a school at Cetinje for the daughters of what, for want of a better term, we may term the upper classes, but has provided for the general education of the youth of the Principality; so that at the present moment there is scarcely a single *pleme* which has not a school for girls as well as for boys.†

---

subject appears to be more earnestly taken up by the present Prince than that of education.'—*Travels in South Slavonic Countries*, vol. ii. pp. 238, 239, 2nd edition.

* Delarue.

† " Avant dix années on ne saura trouver en Tsernogorœ un adolescent ne sachant point lire et écrire, et la Montagne-noire pourra, non sans raison, jeter un coup-d'œil de mépris sur certains Grands Etats vantés pour leur science, leur lit-

The female school at Cetinje—the *Jenski Tzernogorski Institute*—will accommodate forty pupils. It is superintended by a highly accomplished Russian lady, assisted by two efficient governesses. The charge for board and education is what we should consider very small, being only a little more than £20 per annum.* But then money is scarce in Montenegro, and this represents a much larger sum than it would in England.†

Both the Prince and Princess take great interest in the work of education throughout Montenegro, and visit the schools of Cetinje frequently, in order to examine the scholars and to ascertain their progress.‡ In addition to these visitors there is a regular inspector of schools for the whole of Montenegro. Relatively to his means and to the extent of his territory, no prince in Europe has laboured more assiduously nor has spent so much in the work

térature et leur industrie, où le tiers des contingents militaires ignore jusqu'aux premières notions de la lecture et de l'écriture.'—*Le Monténégro Contemporain*, p. 364.

* *Rambles in Istria*, &c., p. 190.

† 'In this particular department of female education Cetinje is a missionary centre. Girls come up from the shores of the *Bocche* for the better instruction which is to be had on the Black Mountain.'—FREEMAN.

‡ LADY STRANGFORD, *Eastern Shores of the Adriatic*, p. 162; MISSES MACKENZIE and IRBY, *Travels in South Slavonic Countries*, vol. ii. p. 239, 2nd edition.

of the education of his people as Prince Nicholas, and every farthing so contributed has been given out of very limited means, and at the cost of much personal sacrifice.*

* At the time of my visit to Montenegro I made the acquaintance of the Archimandrite Nicephorus Doucich, at Cetinje, where I found him busied with the schools of which he was inspector, and interested in the literary questions discussed in the learned societies of Europe. He is a member of the scientific and historical societies of Dalmatia and Serbia, and his contributions to literature are numerous and esteemed. One of his latest publications, ' Tzrna Gora' (Belgrade, 1874), is a valuable contribution to the history of the land tenures, the social organization, and present condition of Montenegro. Of polished, pleasing address, set off by a *physique* which becomes a Montenegrin, he is a remarkable man. When the woes of Herzegovina drove the people into insurrection, he was peaceably pursuing his clerical duties at Belgrade, whither he had gone from Cetinje. From these and his books he rushed at the cry of his country, and has since proved himself one of the ablest of its soldiers. Few troops have been better led; none by a more learned commander.

PART II.

HISTORY OF MONTENEGRO..

CHAPTER XII.

MONTENEGRIN HISTORY UNTIL THE BATTLE OF KOSSOVA.

IN ancient times Montenegro (*Prevalitana*) was comprised in Illyricum, and its history must be sought in that of the province of which it was a portion. It was included in the district of the Labeates, of which Skodra, the Albanian Scutari, was the capital.* After the defeat of Gentius, King of the Illyrians, by Lucius Anicius Paulus, the prætor, in the year 168 B.C., it remained for a while the independent member of a confederacy of small states, but was at length united to the Roman empire by Augustus. The importance in which the line of coast on the eastern shore of the Adriatic was held by the rulers of Italy is evidenced by the number of military stations and colonies which

* 'Scodra in Illyricum marked the limit of the dominion assigned to Octavius in the West and Antonius in the East.'—MERIVALE's *History of Rome*, ch. xxvii.

the jealousy or policy of the Roman Government planted in Dalmatia. Within the Bocche di Cattaro the modern town of Risano recalls the memory of the ancient Rhisinium, or Rhizinium, which gave its name to the whole of the waters of the Gulf of Cattaro (Rhizonicus sinus). The little city of Cattaro itself stands on the site of the old Roman city of Ascrivium, which, in the days of Porphyrogenitus, was known by the name of Decatera, in which the Romans seem to have attempted to preserve the old Illyrian word Cottor, which is the origin of the modern name of the city, Cattaro.*

On the division of the empire into East and West, Montenegro, with the rest of Illyricum, was for a time reckoned in the Eastern empire; but from the time of Honorius to the days of Augustulus (A.D. 496) it was a part of the Western empire On the extinction of the Roman empire in the West, Pannonia, and the various districts on the borders of the Adriatic, reverted to the Eastern, or Byzantine, empire.† Their possession, however, added little to

* WILKINSON, vol. i. p. 381. The ancient Rizona to which Queen Teuta fled (Polybius) is supposed to be represented by the modern Podgoritza, on the river Ribnitza. (*Ib.*)

† 'Quelques années auparavant (421), l'Illyrie orientale avait été mise, malgré la volonté du Pape de Rome, sous la dépendance spirituelle de l'évêque de Constantinople.'—*Les*

the strength of that empire. Tribes of strange barbarians contended with the Greek Emperor for the rich plains of Bulgaria, the forests of Serbia, and the rugged territory which descended to the Adriatic. Unable to control the swarms of invaders who crossed the Danube and the Save to encounter the Roman armies, the Emperor at Constantinople resorted to the policy of former emperors, and invited fresh hordes of barbarians to arrest the progress of those tribes which offered the greatest resistance to the Roman power.

In A.D. 548 we read of an inroad of Slavs in great numbers into Illyria. Though they defeated the Roman armies which attempted to repel their incursions, yet they appear not to have made any permanent settlements at that time. At the invitation of the Emperor Heraclius (A.D. 610—641), however, two Slavonic tribes from beyond the Danube,* the Croats and Serbs, were invited to settle in the countries which lie to the north of the Balkan

---

Slaves Méridionaux, par E. P. DE SAINTE-MARIE. Paris, 1874.

* ' *Slovan, slovjen, slovjan,* tels sont les noms que les Slaves se donnent eux-mêmes depuis l'antiquité, tandis que les auteurs étrangers du moyen âge les appelaient *Slavi, Sclavi, Sclavini, Slavini.* (Voyez Schafarik, § 25 p. 8.)'— E. P. DE SAINTE-MARIE, p. 153.

Mountains and border on the Adriatic, with the expectation that they might be able to check the dangerous power of the Avars, which at that time threatened to overthrow the Imperial Government. These tribes for a time yielded assistance to, and acknowledged the sovereignty of, the Emperor at Byzantium; but overrun, at length, by the Goths, in their devastation of Dalmatia, and deriving no support from the forces of the Empire, Montenegro became a member of the Slav state, or confederation of states, which occupied the area now comprised within the provinces of Free Serbia, Bosnia, Herzegovina, Montenegro, Stara Serbia, and North Albania, having for its seaboard on the Adriatic the line of coast extending from Spalato to Dyrrhachium, the modern Durazzo.

But though practically independent, the supremacy of the Roman empire was not formally rejected by this confederacy, and Serbian Zupans and Bans for a while accepted titles from the Emperor at Constantinople, and at least called themselves his subjects. After the fall, however, of this confederation, Montenegro became an integral part of the Serbian monarchy, which, in addition to the modern principality of the same name, contained, at various periods of its history, Bosnia, most of Bulgaria,

Dalmatia, and Slavonia, and extended beyond the Balkan Mountains to the coast of the Archipelago on the south, to the River Danube on the north, to the Adriatic on the west, and to the Black Sea on the east.

The government of these several states was from the first rather federal than autocratic, with many elements resembling that of the feudal states of Western Europe. Each district was governed by a *Zupan*,* who, whilst independent within his own Zupa, owed obedience to a Grand Zupan, who was elected by the Zupans of the various states. As the area of this confederation was extended, four Grand Zupans were appointed, whose respective jurisdictions answered to the several provinces of Free Serbia, comprising Stara Serbia, Rascia, Bosnia, and Dioclea, in which latter Zupa Montenegro was included.

Montenegro, or the provinces of the Upper Zeta, as the Principality was called, embraced, however,

---

* *Zupa, zupan*—'Zupa means "band," or confederation, and each zupa was simply a confederation of village communities, whose union was represented by a magistrate, or governor, called a zupan.'—EVANS's *Through Bosnia and the Herzegovina*, p. 21. It seems to have meant the territory, or canton, inhabited by a distinct *plemena*, or tribe, which, as before stated, is made up of different cela.—VLAD. YOVANOVITCH on *The Emancipation of the Serbian Nation*, p. 5 Geneva, 1871.

a wider territory than is now known by that name, including within its limits the present country of Herzegovina, whilst to the south it extended to Skodra, on the southern shore of the lake of the same name. The Grand Zupans who governed these provinces were at length superseded by *Bans*, who, with greater power within their own jurisdiction, usually became free from the central authority. These Bans resembled the various kinglets of the Saxon Heptarchy, and, like them, were subordinate, in reality if not formally, to that Ban whose strength of character, or the importance of whose dominions, gave him a controlling power over the rest of the Bans.

In the eleventh century the Emperor of Constantinople, Basil II., a man of a singularly vigorous character, and as unscrupulous as he was vigorous, crushed the Bulgarian kingdom, and reduced the countries, from the Balkan to the Danube, and from the Black Sea to the Adriatic, with hardly any exception, again under the power of the Eastern Empire. From that date the history of these provinces is obscure, and merges in that of the empire, into which they were incorporated. The present principality of Montenegro appears at one time as virtually independent, at other times as a portion of the Bulgarian or the Serbian kingdom. It was girdled by a rugged frontier, and lay remote from the central authority, which for that reason was often unable to assert its claim to the submission of its dependant. The mountain Principality, however, with its harbours on the Adriatic, was of such consequence, that Douka, or Dioclea, its capital, was from time to time the residence of the Kings of Serbia.

In 1050 Michael Boislav, Grand Zupan of Dioclea, made himself King of Serbia, and received investiture from Pope Gregory VII. After a reign of thirty years he died, in 1080, and was succeeded by his son Bodin, who subjected to his authority the Zupans of Bosnia and Rascia. Domestic strife, however, assisted in the decline of this dynasty and of their country, and we find hardly any traces of its existence until the reign of Stephen Nemania* (A.D. 1139—1196). From his accession to the throne of Serbia the history of Montenegro is included in that of the

---

* All the Serbian monarchs assumed the name of Stephen, which was, however, a title rather than a Christian name. Stephen is but the 'possessor of the crown,' or 'conqueror's wreath' (Στέφανος). Lazare Grebelianovic, who succeeded Stephen Ourosh V., is never called Stephen, but then 'he had only the title Knais, prince or despot.' His son was made 'King' by Bajazet, and was therefore a 'Stephen.'

kingdom of which it became an integral portion. A viceroy, however, under the designation of Zupan or Ban, still ruled the province, and resided either at Skodra or Dioclea.

This latter city, the birthplace of Diocletian, was also the seat of an archbishop, within whose jurisdiction Montenegro was situated; and here, in 1199, an important synod for the correction of practical abuses in the Church was held. St. Saba, the great popular saint of the whole Serb family, and the youngest son of Stephen Nemania, resided here. To him the Serbian Church was indebted for the regulation of its hierarchy, and by him the first bishop of Montenegro was appointed. Dioclea was destroyed in the tenth century by Samuel, King of Bulgaria. It rose, however, from its ruins, and was for a time of importance. At present few remains of the city exist, except the lofty wall which surrounded it, some turrets, and fragments of sculpture and pottery. The churchyard of an adjoining village, however, white with its tombstones of purest marble, still retains slices of fluted columns, portions of rich friezes, and elaborate pagan altars overturned; whilst patches of Roman roads, and the remains of two or three noble bridges in the neighbourhood of the city, prove the existence of a considerable population on the southern border of Montenegro in the time of the Roman and Serbian empires. At Podgoritza, on the Turkish side of the frontier, the traveller will find fragments of Latin and Greek inscriptions built into the walls of many of the houses.

Stephen Dushan, who ascended the throne of Serbia in 1334, had held the province of the two Zetas, comprising the whole of the Herzegovina, the present principality of Montenegro, and Albania, as viceroy to his father, Stephen Ourosh IV.* On his accession to the throne of Serbia he made war with the Greek Emperor, and overran Macedonia, Thessaly, and Acarnania. In 1347 he proclaimed himself Emperor of the Serbs, Greeks, and Bulgarians; and, whilst preparing to besiege Constantinople, in order to make it the seat of his empire, he was carried off by fever, December 18, 1355. To arrest the progress of Dushan,

* In Serbian regal genealogy the numeral represents the order of descent or the surname, not the identity of the Christian name; for instance, the late Prince Michel was called the Third, though no other prince had borne this name. He was the third Obrenovic. The present prince is Milan Obrenovic IV., that is, he is the fourth of this family though only the second of his name—Milan. Inacquaintance with this practice has caused a confusion in books which profess to treat of the early history of Montenegro. The present practice of the Principality is in accordance with general usage.

the Greek Emperor had invited the presence and co-operation of the Turks, who swarmed over from Asia to the defence of the Byzantine empire. But not till upwards of thirty years after the death of Dushan was the Serbian empire overthrown on the fatal field of Kossova, June 1, 1389.

This battle was lost nearly five hundred years ago. It is, however, still freshly remembered and plaintively lamented wherever the Serbian race is settled, as though it had been fought but yesterday. It forms the burden of well-nigh half the songs which the Serbian Muse has uttered; and for the loss not of men but of freedom on the plain of Kossova, the red head-dress of every peasant warrior in Montenegro is to this day veiled with a band of black silk.

CHAPTER XIII.

MONTENEGRO AN INDEPENDENT PRINCIPALITY
(1389—1516).

In 1389, the date of the invasion of Serbia by the Turkish army under Amurath I. (Murad), George Balsha,* the second of that name, was the Ban of Montenegro. This prince had married Youvalitza, one of the daughters of Lazar, King of Serbia. When the disastrous result of the battle of Kossova was known to him, whilst he was on his way to join the forces of Lazar, he fell back, and prepared to defend the province which he governed. At this time the territory over which he ruled embraced, in addition to the present principality of Montenegro,

---

* Ducange (*L'Histoire de l'Empire latin de Constantinople*) thinks it probable that the Balsha were descendants of a French family from Baux, in Anjou, who had settled on the coast of Albania two or three generations before the date of the battle of Kossova. Of this, however, he is content with conjecture rather than with probable evidence.

the southern part of Herzegovina, the coast from Ragusa on the north to the mouth of the Drin on the south, comprising therefore the whole of Albania north of that river. Montenegro now became the asylum of those Serbians who preferred exile from their country to submission to the yoke of the Ottomans, and many of the noblest families of the kingdom sought a refuge amidst its almost inaccessible rocks. This fact, were there no other provocation, would have sufficed to direct the attention of the conquerors to this fragment of the subjugated state, and the first Turkish invasion of Montenegro soon followed. In 1394 Balsha was compelled to solicit assistance from the Venetians, and to purchase it by surrendering to the republic the cities of Croia, Durazzo, and Skodra, his capital. The defeat and capture of Bajazet by Timour, in 1402, arrested, however, the Turkish armies, and did more to save Montenegro than any assistance rendered to it by Venice.

On the death of George Balsha, his son, Balsha III., succeeded. He retook from the Venetians Durazzo, Skodra, and the other towns which his father had been compelled to cede to that republic. On his death, a relation of Balsha, Stephen Tzernoïevitj (1423—1450), succeeded as ruler of Montenegro, which, though contracted, still comprehended, in addition to the territories known at present by this name, the strip of land interposed between the western border of the Lake Skodra and the Adriatic as far as the River Bojana, the country to the east of the Lake Skodra as far as the city of that name— the city itself, however, being in the hands of the Venetians—the whole of the islands in the lake, and the shores of the Bocche di Cattaro to the Adriatic.* As Skodra had been ceded to the Venetians, Stephen fortified Jablac, on the north-eastern side of the lake, and made it his capital. Though the wars of the Sultans Murad II. and Mahomed II. in other directions hindered any very active operations against Stephen, yet at this time Montenegro, from which the Herzegovina had been torn, seemed fast sinking like the surrounding states into vassalage to the Ottoman.

* 'In the interval from 1424 to 1436 the Montenegrins fought no less than sixty-three battles against the Turks, and the latter were sixty-three times beaten.'—*La Souveraineté du Monténégro*, par JEAN VACLIK, Paris, 1858. Such constant warfare must have destroyed the handful of men which was found in Montenegro at the period, even though always victors, but for one circumstance : Montenegro was an asylum open to all who preferred independence to submission to the Turk. Thus its population was replenished, and the number of the people who found shelter there and fought its battles was only limited by the capabilities of the soil.

The Albanian war, and the heroic exploits of George Castriotes, or Scanderbeg, awoke the slumbering spirit of prince and people. Stephen—who had married Valsava, either the sister or the daughter of Castriotes, for authorities differ as to the actual relationship of his wife to Scanderbeg—joined the army of the Albanian hero with a Montenegrin contingent, and by his side shared in the dangers of the long campaign (1450—1490). He lies buried in one of the islets on the Lake of Skodra. In acknowledgment of services rendered to the republic of Venice in the defence of her Albanian possessions, he was made a patrician of that city, and in 1474 his name was inscribed in the Golden Book of the republic. Ivan (John) the Black, eldest of the three sons of Stephen, succeeded his father, and at first in conjunction with his brother George, and after his death, alone, governed Montenegro.

Up to the accession of Ivan, the Zupan, or prince, who led the soldiers of the Principality was vigorously employed in keeping the forces of the enemy at a distance from the present territory of Montenegro. He was closely occupied in warfare, just as his successors since, but it was warfare on the whole forced upon him to prevent the barbarian from invading his dominion, not warfare to repel an actual invader. Now properly commenced the history of Montenegro, and that series of assaults upon Montenegro itself which has lasted to our own times, and which has called forth all the skill and strength of ruler and people to preserve their narrow territory from being swallowed up by the all-devouring armies of Turkey. In 1453 the small remnants of the Eastern empire, which had shrunk to a corner of Thrace, were taken, together with Constantinople, its capital. In 1459, seventy years after the battle of Kossova, Serbia ceased to be a tributary principality, and became an Ottoman province; and in the same year, on the death of Scanderbeg, Albania submitted to the same power, or at any rate ceased from active resistance. Six years later, in 1463, Bosnia was overrun by the Turks, and incorporated into their empire. In 1476 the Herzegovina was subdued; and Montenegro, hemmed in on all sides by Turkish territory, and consisting only of a handful of men, was compelled to wage a seemingly hopeless contest for its bare existence. That existence was the more necessary now, not only for the sake of her own sons, but still more for the sake of the suffering people of the subjugated states along her frontiers, since the rocky citadel which Nature had heaped up, as though to be the refuge from oppression, was the only asylum open to those Serbs who preferred freedom, though attended with heavy privations, to submission to the Ottoman rule.

The heroism of this handful of men—for every Montenegrin woman and child possessed a man's heart—rose with the occasion which demanded its exercise. The spirit which animated their Prince was exhibited by the whole Montenegrin people in their now hourly struggles against the Turks, and is well illustrated by a unanimous decree of the assembled Principality. In this it was first enacted that, in time of war against the common enemy, no Montenegrin should on any pretext quit the field of battle without the express order of the Prince. That he who should turn his back upon the enemy, and attempt to seek safety in flight, should be for ever disgraced, and treated with every mark of contempt; and then, dressed in woman's garments, and armed with a spindle instead of a sword, he should be turned out of his home, and beaten by women armed with the same implements. Finally, he was to be driven to the frontiers as a coward and traitor to the cause of Montenegrin liberty. So long as such a spirit animated prince and people—and it still animates them—cowardice must have been all but unknown, and regard for mere personal safety generally disregarded.* It would be too much to assert that no acts of cowardice have occurred in Montenegro since the time that this law was promulgated. All that can be said is that no such act of cowardice as is here stigmatized has been recorded in song or tradition during four centuries of warfare.

Finding Jablac to be no longer tenable, and being refused the assistance of the Venetians, who dreaded the injury to their commercial interests from the vengeance of Mahomet II., Ivan retired from that city, and, having burnt it, took refuge in Cetinje, which from that moment has remained the capital of Montenegro, the seat of its bishop, and the residence of its princes.† Here he built a monastery,

---

* By the 18th article of the Code Danilo it is declared that if any one shall refuse to take up arms or hesitate to march against the enemy, he shall be deprived of his arms, never be allowed to wear them again, shall be stripped of any honour he may have received, and be compelled to wear a woman's apron in proof that he has not the heart of a man. (E gli verrà inoltre cinto un grembiule in contrassegno della mancanza in lui d'un cuore virile.)

† 'Au règne d'Ivan, c'est-à-dire vers l'an 1480, commence l'histoire distincte du Monténégro ; jusque-là elle est confondue avec celle des principautés auxquelles ce petit pays était adjoint ; jusque-là son sol n'était, en grande partie, occupé que par des pâtres. De là vient le nom de Katunska appliqué à l'un de ses principaux districts, et qui

and made the city the see of the Metropolitan of the Zeta. On the Obod, the name of the river which is now known by the name of the Tzrnoievitza Rjeka, he erected a fortress to check any advance of the Turks into Montenegro from that quarter, and established at the same time, under the protection of its walls, the first printing-office erected in these countries. The types, which have never been exceeded in beauty, were procured by him from Venice; and from this press the first copies of various volumes of the Slavonic Liturgy were issued. Here, five years after his retreat, he died, and was buried in the monastery which he had founded in that city. Under the familiar designation of Ivan Beg, the popular songs of the time abound with tales of his exploits, and he is still the most popular hero of the South Slavs, and 'his memory survives as freshly in the mountains as though he had died but yesterday. Springs, ruins, caverns are called after his name, Ivan Begova, and it is hoped that he will reappear one day as a celestial liberator or political Messiah.' * In 1490, on the death of Ivan, he was succeeded by his son George, who married

signifie *cabanes de bergers.*'—*Lettres sur l'Adriatique et Monténégro,* par X. MARMIER, t. ii. p. 136.

* Cyprien Robert, t. i. p. 129.

Elizabeth Erizza, of a noble Venetian family. In the struggle against the Turks, domestic trouble was added to foreign invasion. His brother Stanicha, or Stephen, having apostatized, and received assistance from Bajazet II., led an army of Turks and renegade Montenegrins against his brother and his native country. In this attempt he was defeated. The lives, however, of the Montenegrin apostates were spared, and on their submission they were allowed to settle in the country. This permission led to troubles at a subsequent period. Stanicha himself attempted to fix his residence at Skodra, which was assigned to him by the Sultan. The inhabitants of that city, however, refusing to permit him to do so, he retired to the village of Bouchati, in Albania, and from thence his descendants were known as the Bouchatlia—a name not yet extinct. Notwithstanding the necessity which then, as now, compelled a Prince of Montenegro to be in continual warfare with the armies of Turkey, this Prince devoted every moment, when not engaged in actual warfare, to the intellectual improvement of his subjects. Almost before any other European sovereign had interested himself in the advancement of popular education, George IV. of Montenegro had exerted himself in the cause of education and in the erection of schools throughout his rugged Principality. The marriage of Prince George led to a great evil: the contrast between the gaieties of Venice, where his wife possessed a house, and the dangers, and still more the austerity, of her mountain life, made her regret her paternal home, and the visits of George and his wife to that city grew more and more prolonged, and his absence from Montenegro more frequent, until at length it became a practice in his house which paved the way for the ready abdication of his successor. According to the annals of the Principality, George IV. was succeeded by his son Stephen, of whom nothing more is recorded than that he reigned only a short time. His son Ivan, who succeeded him, reigned, it is said, but a few months, and his son George V. succeeded. This prince, the last of the dynasty of Tzrnoievic, abandoned his sterile home in 1516, and took up his abode, first at Venice, and, when this retreat became unsafe, in France. He migrated to Rome, and at length settled at Constantinople, where part of his family apostatized from Christianity. At the same time that the Prince left Montenegro, many of the chief families of the Principality deserted their homes, not unnaturally tired, as it would seem, of these sterile lands; and, hopeless of resistance to the advance of the Ottoman power, at length finally abandoned Montenegro.

Of this period of the history of the Principality and of its alliance with Venice, Cyprien Robert remarks, that 'from the moment when Venice, in the height of its greatness, courted the alliance of Ivan, the Tzrnogorski never ceased to serve the whole of Northern Italy as a bulwark against the Turks, who, having become masters of Bosnia and Albania since the death of Scanderbeg, would certainly have put an end to the republic of St. Mark but for the Slav corsairs and haiduks* that lined the eastern shores of the Adriatic.'† The safety of Italy was secured by the heroism of Montenegro, and Mahomet II. was checked in his expeditions, by which he hoped to overthrow Venice and to conquer Naples, by the unflinching resistance of these mountaineers.

* Partizans engaged in warfare by land as privateers by sea.
† 'Les Slaves de Turquie,' t. i. p. 429.

CHAPTER XIV.

THE LEGEND OF STANICHA.

WHETHER of the two sons of Ivan Beg, George, who succeeded his father, or Stanicha, who apostatized to the faith of Mahomet, were the elder is matter of uncertainty. It is, however, probable that George was the younger, and that his brother forfeited the right to succeed to the rule of the Principality by abandoning the Christian religion.* The grounds for the apostacy are detailed in several *piesmas* which are still sung, not only in Montenegro, but throughout the other Serb lands which border on the Danube. These songs, there can be but little doubt, have preserved the records of events in history, however heightened and disfigured they may possibly be by the fancies of the bards to whom we are indebted for their preservation.

* Stanicha, or Stephen, is sometimes called Maximus, a name given him possibly to denote that he was the elder.

According to these history-ballads Ivan Beg, in his visit to Venice in 1483, undertaken for the purpose of urging the obligations of the treaties made between Montenegro and the republic of St. Mark, had sought for each of his sons a wife from among the influential patrician families of that city. George was eventually married to a daughter of the Erizzi, whilst Stanicha was betrothed to a daughter of the Doge Mocenigo, who had been the companion of Ivan in the deliverance of Skodra when besieged by the Turks. The romantic incident of this ill-omened betrothal of the Orthodox prince with a Latin bride, and its consequences to Montenegro, can, however, best be told in the language of the original piesmas.

'The Tzrnoievic Ivo writes a letter to the Doge of great Venice: "Hearken to me Doge! as they say that thou hast in thy house the most beautiful of roses, so there is in my house the handsomest of pinks. Doge, let us unite the rose with the pink." The Venetian Doge replies in flattering terms; Ivo repairs to his court, taking with him three loads of gold, in order to woo the fair Latin in his son's name. When he had lavished all his gold, the Latins agreed with him that the wedding should take place at the next vintage. Ivo, who was wise, yet uttered foolish words at his departure: "Friend and Doge," said he, "thou shalt soon see me again, with six hundred choice companions; and if there is among them a single one who is handsomer than my son Stanicha, give me neither dower nor bride." The delighted Doge pressed his hand, and presented him with the apple of gold,* and Ivo returned to his country.

'He was approaching his castle of Jablac, when from the *koula*, with its elegant balconies, and its glazed windows glittering in the sun, his faithful consort perceived him. Instantly she flies to meet him on the Livada, covers the hem of his mantle with kisses, presses his terrible weapons to her heart, carries them with her own hands into the castle, and has a silver chair placed for the hero. The winter passed off cheerfully; but in the spring, Stanicha was seized with the small-pox, which pitted his face all over. When the old man assembled his six hundred *Svati*, or boon companions, at the approach of autumn, it was easy for him, alas! to find among them a warrior handsomer than his son.

---

* Among the Slavo-Greek people, the apple is to this day the symbol of wedlock and beauty, as in the time of Helen and the shepherd Paris.

Then his forehead was gathered into wrinkles, and *the black moustaches that reached his shoulders grew limp.*

'His wife, having learned the cause of his grief, upbraided him with the pride that had made him wish to ally himself with the superb Latins. Stung by her reproaches, Ivo burned with wrath; he would hear no more of the wedding, and sent the Svati away. Long time elapsed: when suddenly came a ship with a message from the Doge: the letter fell on Ivo's knees. It said: "When thou enclosest a meadow with hedges, thou mowest it, or thou leavest it to another, that the snows of winter may not spoil its flourishing grass. When one asks for a fair one in marriage, and obtains her, one should come and fetch her, or write to her that she is free to form a new engagement."

'Jealous of keeping his word, Ivo determines at last to go to Venice; he assembles all his noble brethren in arms from Dulcigno and from Antivari, the Drekalovic, the Koutchi, and the Bratonojic, the falcons of Podgoritza and Bielopavlic, the Vassojevic, and all the young men as far as to the green Lim. He takes heed that the Yunaks* come each in the costume peculiar to his tribe, and that

* Warriors.

all are dressed as sumptuously as possible. He is resolved, he says, that the Latins shall be in ecstasies when they behold the magnificence of the Serbs. They have many fine things, those noble Latins! they know how to work metals with skill, and to weave precious stuffs: but they lack what is more worthy of envy; they have not the lofty brow and the commanding look of the Tzrnogorski.

'Seeing the six hundred Svati assembled, Ivo relates to them the imprudent promise he had made to the Doge, and the punishment inflicted on him by Heaven, in the person of his son, smitten with small-pox. "What say you, brothers?" said he, "shall we put one of you in place of Stanicha during the journey, and leave him, on our return, half the presents which will be made to him as the real bridegroom?" All the Svati approved of this stratagem, and the young Voivode of Dulcigno, Obrenovo Djuro, having been declared the handsomest in the assembly, was requested to accept the feigned part. Djuro refused for a long time, and was only prevailed on to consent by the most sumptuous gifts. Then the Svati embarked, crowned with flowers; and were saluted on their departure by the whole artillery of the Black Mountain, and by the two enormous cannons named *Kernio* and

Selenko, which have not their match in the seven Frank kingdoms, nor among the Turks: the mere report of these pieces makes coursers bend the knee, and knocks down many a hero.

'Arrived at Venice, the Tzrnogorski stop at the ducal palace. The festivities of the betrothal last a whole week, at the end of which Ivo exclaims, "Friend Doge, we must back to our mountains." The Doge then rising, asks his guests where is the bridegroom Stanicha; they all point to Djuro. The Doge then gives Djuro the kiss and the golden apple of wedlock. The Doge's two sons then advance, bringing two damasked fusils of the value of a thousand ducats; they ask where is Stanicha, and all the Svati show them Djuro. The two Venetians embrace him as their brother-in-law, and deliver their presents to him. After them come the Doge's two sisters-in-law, bringing two shirts of the finest linen, all wrought with gold; they ask which is the bridegroom, and all the Svati point with their fingers to Djuro. Satisfied with their stratagem, Ivo and the Tzrnogorski took their way back to their country.'

On arriving at her destined home, the piesma goes on to tell that the bride was soon undeceived. Instead of the handsome Voivode to whom she had been bethrothed she was presented to a husband disfigured with the scars of the small-pox, and repulsive from the wasting disease which had followed upon the original disorder. A prince, however, at worst is a prince, and the republican damsel seems to have easily reconciled herself to the momentary disappointment, and to have made but little difficulty in giving up the blooming proxy for the wasted princelet. One surrender, however, was not so easy. Half the bridal presents, according to the agreement of Ivan, was to remain in the possession of the Voivode and was to be the payment for his share in the stratagem by which the bride was lured from Venice. These she had not the heart to relinquish. The surrender of a husband was one matter, to give up so much of the 'costly array and broidered apparel' at the same time was another.

' "I cannot," she cries to Stanicha, weeping for vexation, "I cannot surrender that marvellous tunic of gold, embroidered by my own hands, under which I dreamed of caressing my spouse, and which nearly cost me both my eyes, by working at it night and day for three years. Though a thousand broken shafts of lances should form thy bier, my Stanicha, thou must fight to recover it; or if thou dare not, I will turn my courser's bridle, and hurry him to the sea-shore. There I will pluck a leaf of aloes; I will scratch my face with its thorns, and drawing blood from my cheeks, I will write with that blood a letter which my falcon will carry swiftly to great Venice, whence my faithful Latins will hasten to avenge me." At these words of the daughter of Venice, Stanicha can no longer control himself; with his whip of three lashes he smites his black courser, which bounds like a tiger, and having come up with Djuro, the Tzrnogorski pierces him with his javelin through the middle of the forehead. The handsome Voivode falls dead at the foot of the mountain.

'Petrified with horror, all the Svati stared at each other for a while; at last their blood began to boil, and they exchanged pledges—terrible pledges —which were not now those of friendship, but of fury and death. All day the chiefs of the tribes fought one against the other, until their ammunition was spent, and night had added its darkness to the bloody reek of the field of battle. The few survivors walk up to their knees in the blood of the dead. See with what difficulty an old man advances! That hero, so changed in appearance, is the Tzrnoievic Ivo; in his irremediable woe he invokes the Lord: "Send me a wind from the mountain, and disperse this horrible fog, that I may see which of my people has survived." Moved by his prayer, God sent a blast of wind that swept the air. Ivo could see the whole plain covered afar with horses and riders cut in pieces, and the old man went about from one heap of slain to another, looking for his son.

'Yovan, one of Ivo's nephews, who lay dying, saw him pass, and, collecting his strength, raised himself on his elbow, and cried out, "Halloa, uncle Ivo! how proudly thou passest, without asking thy nephew if the wounds he has received for thee are deep. What makes thee so disdainful? Is it the presents of the fair Latin?" Ivo turns back at these words, and, bursting into tears, asks the Tzrnogorski Yovan how his son Stanicha died. "He is alive," replied Yovan; "he is fleeing towards Jablac on his swift steed, and the repudiated daughter of Venice is going back a virgin to her father."'

Flying from the vengeance of the clansmen of the murdered Voivode, and from the execrations of those who, but for this murder, would have been his future subjects, Stanicha escaped with a few personal followers to the Turkish fortress of Jablac, and afterwards retired to Constantinople. Here he embraced

Islamism, and soon sought means to recover his share of the family possessions and his right to rule over the Principality. The aid of the Sultan was readily given for this purpose, though he happily failed to attain what would have rendered Montenegro tributary to the Turkish power, and eventually a part of the empire. Stanicha, however, long remained a standing menace and a source of danger to his native country. After being defeated in an invasion of the Principality he settled first at Skodra, and, when driven out by the people of that city, then at Bouchati in Albania, where his children remained invested with a certain rank and authority, until in 1833 the last of the known descendants of Ivan Beg, Mustapha Pasha, was exiled by the Porte.

One unhappy consequence resulted from this murder; it was one, if not the chief, cause of the separation which has existed from that time between the mountaineers of Albania and those of Montenegro. This separation was effected—the course of the present war forbids me to say permanently—by the acceptance on the part of the Mirdites and Albanian clans of the Latin rite, whilst the Montenegrins have remained zealous adherents of the Orthodox Eastern Church.

CHAPTER XV.

MONTENEGRO UNDER THE PRINCE-BISHOPS: PERIOD THE FIRST, ELECTIVE BISHOPS (A.D. 1516—1696.)

On the retirement of the last of its hereditary princes, the Bishop, not only by the appointment of George V., but as the next important person in the Principality, became, first the regent, and, on the final renunciation of the duties of his station by the secular prince, the actual ruler of Montenegro; and for one hundred and eighty years the government was directed—like some of the provinces of Germany—by a prince-bishop. Unlike the bishops, however, who succeeded to that office after the year 1696, these ecclesiastical governors either confined themselves to the spiritual duties of their office, or at any rate subordinated their civil functions to those of their episcopal duties. In order to assist the "Vladika" in the government of the Principality, a governor was appointed, to whose care was assigned all matters concerning the military array and defence of the country, yet with a certain inferiority of position to the Bishop himself. This civil governor was always the "obor knes," or Voivode of the Katunska nahia, the cradle and citadel of Montenegrin independence. In all spiritual matters, however, the Bishop owed obedience to the Serbian Patriarch of Ipek, who was expected to visit the territory of his suffragan once in seven years, and whose right it was to consecrate the bishops of Montenegro.

We learn, from the imprint of books printed in Montenegro, that at the time of the abdication of the secular Prince, Vavyl, or Babylas, who had been consecrated to the office of bishop in the time of George IV., was the first episcopal regent. On his death, shortly after this event, German was elected, in 1520, to succeed him, and his episcopate was signalized by the recommencement of the struggle between Turkey and Montenegro. To this the Turks were encouraged by the favourable circumstances of the times. Montenegro in fact had come to be divided into two camps. If hereditary principles were to be regarded, and they had great weight, Stanicha, the renegade, was the rightful heir to chief power within the Principality. Although he had been defeated at Liekopolje, on the Moratcha, when, in the reign of his brother, he led a force composed of Turks and his Montenegrin followers against his country, he had never relinquished the hope of occupying the position of his father at Cetinje. His followers, though renegades for the most part like himself, had on their defeat been allowed to reoccupy their possessions in Montenegro, and these were at that time, and long remained, a source of weakness and of positive danger to their country. Despising, then, the pacific duties and character of the new ruler, the Pasha of Skodra, availing himself of the divisions in the country, with a large army of Turks and renegades, made a desperate effort to subjugate the Principality. In this attempt he was defeated with heavy loss, and Montenegro obtained unwonted rest for several years. The season of repose was prolonged in consequence of the employment of the Turkish forces in their struggle against the Hungarians, who had invaded Bosnia. This period is memorable for the expedition undertaken to serve the common cause indeed, but at a distance from the frontiers of the Principality. In the struggle Ivan Voukotic, the civil governor of Montenegro, rendered effectual assistance for a time to the Hungarian troops besieged by the Turks at

Jajeze, and in a fiercely contested battle the Turkish army was defeated with great slaughter.

The repose which, on the whole, Montenegro enjoyed at this period is attributed in some degree to the policy of the Sultan. To all appearance a few years of such rest would end in transferring the rule of the Principality to the Turks. Montenegro seemed to be gradually lapsing into a Turkish province. The population was becoming infiltrated with Mussulman settlers, in part the descendants of the renegades, in part emigrants from the neighbouring provinces of Turkey. As all these enjoyed toleration, and Montenegro was an asylum against fiscal exaction and wrong, it was sought alike by Christians and Mussulmans. But for the impatience of the Turkish authorities, the history of Montenegro might have been as cheerless as that of the other provinces of the old Serbian empire. Tired, however, of waiting for the gradual decay of the Christian power, or relying in the strength of the Mussulman settlers, the Turks in 1570 renewed the war with this people.

This invasion lasted for several years, and the frontiers were so insecure, that on the death of the Bishop, which took place soon after the war had recommenced, his successor was unable to proceed to Ipek for consecration, nor could the Patriarch of that city make his usual visitation of Montenegro, and perform the act of consecration at Cetinje. Favoured by the state of uncertainty and confusion, and by the number of renegades scattered throughout the country, Ali, Pasha of Skodra, overran great part of the country, and compelled the portions of which he held momentary possession to pay tribute to the Sultan. In the war the printing-press which Ivan Beg and his son George IV. had introduced was destroyed and the types dispersed; but whether these were destroyed by the Turks, or melted down by the Montenegrins into bullets in defence of Rjeka, is uncertain. What is certain is, that from that time until the days of Peter II. no printing was executed in Montenegro, and the few who learned to read within its borders had to turn to foreign sources for the books which they required.

This period of distress was rendered more calamitous to Montenegro by the falling away of the Koutchi and other tribes of the Berda from the Orthodox Eastern Church, and their submission to the Roman See. This was effected by the labours of Latin missionaries sent from the Propaganda at Rome. This religious separation destroyed the political and national unity of these people, and was the cause of many subsequent misfortunes to both parties. Montenegro was weakened by the schism, and the Koutchi and the other Roman Catholic tribes, whether Slavs or Albanians, fell under the dominion of Turkey.

In 1604 the Montenegrins refused any longer to pay the tribute which had been imposed upon them, and expelled the Turkish garrison which had been left to overawe them; and on the advance of the Turkish force to compel them to submission, they defeated the army sent for that purpose. In the battles which took place on the banks of the Moratcha the Turks suffered a great loss, and Ali, the Pasha of Skodra, who commanded, escaped sorely wounded from the field. At this time, as we know from the Venetian relation, the whole number of the combatants belonging to the Principality was 8,027. These, with the help received from their wives and sisters, were the warriors who foiled the ablest generals of the Ottoman, and prevented the Sultan from hurling his armies on the coast of Italy, at a moment when, in all human probability, but for this diversion, he must have succeeded. In this war the Montenegrins fought on horseback, and their victories were now gained, in hand-to-hand fights, by a motley army of armed men, fighting with the handjar, cross-bow, the occasional musquet, but, above all, with the stones, which they rolled down from their almost inaccessible heights upon the heads of their invaders. The result was that the Turks were everywhere chased from Montenegro with heavy losses, both of men and arms: the last item being of the utmost importance to the conquerors, since it gave the mountaineers that which they so much needed—weapons wherewith to resist in any future invasions. For, in the absence of arsenals and military stores, the Montenegrin people have always depended upon the arms which the Turkish fugitives have thrown away in their flight, or the slain have left upon the field of battle.

The next year a new governor of Albania, Arstan Pasha, advanced at the head of 60,000 Turks to avenge the defeat of his predecessor. Under these disproportionate odds the Montenegrins sought and received the assistance of some of the neighbouring tribes, and about 10,000 men assembled to repel the new invasion. From April until far in the month of September war rolled around the southern frontier. On the 10th of the latter month the Turkish commander encountered the Montenegrin army on the plain of Lieko, where Stanicha had been defeated by his nephew, Stephen II., in the early part of the century. The battle was a decisive one. After a short but sanguinary engagement the main body of the enemy broke and fled, leaving the field strewn with the bodies of the Turkish soldiers. Among the heads carried off and exhibited on the tower at Cetinje was that of the Pasha's lieutenant.

The blow was felt at least along the whole frontier, and the departure of the Turkish army brought a short cessation of hostilities to the Montenegrins. The clash of arms was suspended, whilst a singular project was formed, which, though dictated primarily by personal ambition and private aims, recalls the policy and memory of the Crusades. Margaret, one of the last descendants of the Paleologi, had years before married Frederick, the first Duke of Mantua. His grandson, Charles, Duke of Nevers and of Rethel, was now the sole representative, and, what was more, the sole recognised heir of the Paleologi. He conceived the not unnatural scheme of a combination of European powers to restrain the dreaded power of the Sultan, to expel the Turkish troops from Europe, and as a result to seat the heir of the Paleologi upon the imperial throne of his fathers. Ships were bought, troops were to be levied, money was promised, the Pope was to bestow his future blessing upon the expedition, and gave his present encouragement to the scheme. Albania and Montenegro were reckoned upon as factors in the campaign to come, and the great Cardinal Richelieu lent support to the intended crusade. Agents acknowledged and unacknowledged flitted from court to court; soldiers of fortune pledged their swords, in consideration of the pay they were to receive; and—all ended in smoke. Whilst, however, the scheme was a possibility, Turkey was too much occupied to consider its small hereditary foe. Montenegro obtained a short respite from war, and the annals of the little Principality are barren of events of general interest.

No sooner, however, had the alarm of this attack upon his European provinces ceased, than the Sultan resumed his war with Montenegro. An expedition was planned, formidable from the forces engaged and the determination evinced of at length crushing at all hazards the resistance of these people, and destroying them by the mere force of numbers, without regard to any losses that might accrue to the invaders. The army of Turkey, under the command of Suleiman, Pasha of Skodra, was led to the southern frontier of this country. A battle ensued, which is said to have lasted twenty days, nightfall only separating the combatants. In this long conflict or series of engagements, though the arms of Turkey gained no honour, the Montenegrins, unable to recruit their numbers, and overwhelmed by the fresh troops which were daily brought up and opposed to them, were compelled to fall back. Cetinje itself was now occupied and the convent plundered, while those who resisted were put to the sword. Those who submitted to the Turks were compelled to pay the haratch; whilst those who refused to submit took shelter in the broken ground along the Lovchen Mountain, and harrassed the invaders from their vantage-ground. Again the Turkish commander retired from this inhospitable country, where a small army was useless, where a large army was certain to be starved. Small garrisons, however, were left behind, which were to hold the country in subjection. His retirement was the signal for the reappearance of the soldiers who had sought a refuge in the heights around Cetinje, and who commenced attacking these garrisons, and preventing any supplies reaching them, as soon as the main body was out of sight; whilst the various tribes which inhabited the Berda and the adjacent fastnesses of Albania, especially the Koutchi and Clementi, sallied out, and attacking the retiring army unexpectedly in the neighbourhood of Podgoritza, almost totally destroyed it. Again the expedition of Turkey was an ignominious failure, attended with the destruction of the army destined to effect the conquest of Montenegro.

The destruction of much of the sympathy which existed between the Albanian tribes south of Skodra and the Montenegrins to the north of that city, through their separation into the two camps of Orthodox and Catholic, has been a fertile cause of disaster to both. At the very time when the closest unity was necessary, division was introduced by the passing over of one portion of the Albanian Slaves from the Eastern to the Western Church. The latter turned for protection to France, and at that time the protection was not accorded, except at the price of abandoning their religious convictions, together with much which constituted national life. Another evil was impending: the protection accorded by France to the one body was to be met by protection accorded by Russia to its own co-religionists, and the jealousies of Europe and subsequent wars have been the result. Undivided, these tribes might have relied on their own powers of resistance and the defensive strength of their territory; divided, they have been unable to protect themselves, which, but for this division, they might have done. During the invasion of Montenegro the Turks were allowed by the Albanian tribes for the most part to crush the resistance of their neighbours of the Black Mountain; and it was only when this was accomplished that the Clementi awoke to the danger which menaced themselves. It was, however, too late. Their country was overrun, and they were crushed in their turn, though not without terrible loss to their Turkish invaders, and also not without examples of the most heroic courage on the part of the Clementi.

To return, however, to the people of Montenegro. The main body of the Turkish army had no sooner withdrawn from Cetinje, where it was impossible for them to find food, than the bands which had taken shelter in the unassailable parts of the Katunska nahia swarmed down from the heights of the Lovchen and from the crests which surround Niegush, and drove the Turkish garrisons from their posts. Nor was the Sultan able at that moment to chastise these assailants. All his available forces were then engaged in the siege of Vienna or in maintaining his communications with the army encamped before that city, and Montenegro was able to free itself from the presence of the Turkish troops.

In 1687 the Venetian republic proposed an alliance with Montenegro, in order to induce these people to attack the Turkish posts lying on the northern frontier of the Principality, and thus cause a diversion which would prevent the Turks from concentrating their troops in the Morea, which country was then being invaded by the Venetians. But though the Montenegrins, true to their instinct of combating the Turks at all times, responded to the call of the republic of Venice, they failed to procure that return in the hour of their own necessity which had been promised them, and which they had a right to expect.

In 1688 the Turkish Government made another energetic effort to reduce these people to subjection. The struggle was desperate, and the Turks were beaten in a sanguinary engagement at the foot of Mount Vertielki. Meanwhile another column of the Ottoman army had already penetrated to Cetinje. Hopeless of succour, and determined not to fall into the hands of the Turks, the monks who occupied the monastery which Ivan Beg had built threw their treasures, their plate, and their books into the wells or other secret places, and then blowing up the monastery, perished in the destruction of the building.

In the course of the ensuing year the Emperor Leopold sought the alliance of the Montenegrins, and prevailed upon them to co-operate with his troops in the campaign against the Turks of Bosnia and Serbia. The armies of the Emperor, however, were unsuccessful, and as usual the Montenegrins found themselves deserted, and were again exposed to the fury of the Turks. At the peace of Carlowitz which followed, Austria, Russia, and Venice made stipulations in their own interests with the Porte; but the ally whom all had found useful in the hour of their struggle against Turkey was unnamed in the treaty which was then made, and Montenegro was abandoned to the vindictive assaults of the Ottoman. During the whole of this period of one hundred and eighty years, though Montenegro was governed by its bishops, assisted by a civil governor, we only obtain an occasional glimpse of these rulers. The whole period was one continued national struggle, in which every man, armed with his own weapons, fighting at his own cost, and relying upon his own bravery, warred against the enemies of his religion and his freedom. At a later period the chieftains present a stronger individuality, but for the period comprised in this chapter it will suffice if I subjoin a list of the Vladikas in the order of their succession:—

Babylas, Macarias,* German (1520), Rubin, or Rufim, Pa. Koman, M. Korpetchani, Rubin Veliakraïski, Basil, Visarion Baïtcha (1687), Sava Kalugeric.†

* *Geschichte des Fürstenthums Montenegro.* Von ALEXANDER ANDRIE. Wien, 1853, p. 18.

† *Les Slaves Méridionaux, leur origine et leur établissement dans l'ancienne Illyrie,* p. 162.

CHAPTER XVI.

HEREDITARY PRINCE-BISHOPS (1697).—DANILO PETROVIC.

THE election of a ruler over a nation in which every member claims the same rights and performs the same duties, is attended with inconveniences and dangers which no advantages arising out of the free choice of a governor can ever compensate. This practice convulsed and eventually destroyed Poland; it threatened to overthrow the freedom of Montenegro. At the close of the seventeenth century, however, a change took place which enabled these people to consolidate their power, to concentrate their energies, and successfully to defend their independence without losing any portion of their old liberty. They agreed to abolish the elective episcopacy, and to substitute an hereditary one in its place. Montenegro, reduced within the straitest limits, seemed, at this date, on the point of becoming subject to Turkey.

Before the first years of the eighteenth century the small principality of Montenegro was almost entirely comprised within the limits of the two nahias of Katunska and Rjeka. Of these, Rjeka was in part occupied by families of renegades, whose allegiance was divided between attachment to their race and obedience to their religion, whilst the whole of the Katunska nahia east of Cetinje had been held, overrun, and reduced to more than its normal desolation by the Turks. If Montenegro is to be regarded as a fortress, the country between Cetinje and Cattaro may be considered as the citadel of its independence. This district has never been penetrated by an enemy, and hither the strongest and most active of the people have always fled for shelter, and from it have sallied forth to harass the Turks until they were compelled to retire, when the Montenegrins have always returned and reoccupied their old homes. Towards the centre of this impenetrable district is the village of Niegush, the site of which had, at the close of the seventeenth century, been occupied for about two hundred years by families who had fled from the Turks, when the Herzegovina submitted to their rule. These settlers had given to the grey rocky solitude where they had found refuge the name of their native village.

Among the families settled at Niegush, one of the most influential was that of Petrovic, and from the house of that family the people chose their new Bishop. Strenuously did Danilo Petrovic refuse the proffered office. The times demanded a man of iron will, of clear head, and large influence. He was but young, too young he deemed himself to be for the important office. Long he refused to comply with the wishes of the people. At length their importunity conquered, and he consented to be the new Vladika. This happened in 1697. It was not, however, until full three years after, 1700, that he could be consecrated to this office.

As the bishops throughout the Orthodox Eastern Church are unmarried, the succession could not, therefore, devolve in the right line, and the people of Montenegro having experienced the inconvenience of an elective sovereignty, now authorised the Vladika to recommend his successor from among the members of his own family. It is true that the people still retained their right to elect their Prince. They exercised this right by consenting to receive the person recommended to them by the testament of the Vladika. The rule of a prince-bishop and their right of nominating a successor to the people for election ended at the accession of

Prince Danilo in 1851, having at that time continued upwards of one hundred and fifty years. From that time the succession was settled by the act of the Skupschina.

Most writers say that from the time of his election the thoughts of the new Vladika were directed towards finding means to rid Montenegro of its great source of weakness, the presence of the renegades, who, dwelling in various parts of the Principality, aided the enemy in his attempts to subjugate the country. For this there seems no grounds except conjecture, and the evident necessity for some such action. Be that as it may, whether this determination was suggested by, or was merely accelerated by, the conduct of the Pasha of Skodra, it followed hard upon an act of treachery but too common in the history of the Ottomans.

In 1702, whilst Demir Pasha was governor of Skodra, the people of the Lower Zeta, included within the episcopal jurisdiction of the Montenegrin prelate, and still inhabited largely by Christians, had built a church, which they desired should be consecrated by their bishop. As it was dangerous to adventure upon Turkish territory for this purpose, Danilo hesitated to comply with their wishes. To remove his objection, the people purchased from the

Pasha a safe conduct for him whilst engaged in this duty. Still he hesitated, declaring that he had no faith in Turkish promises. After a while, however, moved by the importunity of the people, and secured, as they thought, by the solemn promises of the Pasha, Danilo visited the Zeta, and consecrated the church without molestation. No sooner, however, had he performed this duty than he was seized, and, in spite of the promises of safety, thrown into prison and there tortured.

From prison the Vladika was brought forth to death; and to make this death more terrible and more significant he was condemned to be crucified. In order, moreover, that no circumstance should be wanting to make this a real martyrdom, in imitation of the death of his Divine Master, he was compelled to drag the wood of which the lofty cross was to be composed to the place of execution. The cross was to be erected close to the Montenegrin frontier, so that he might die in the face of the whole of the people of the mountains. Over the arid, treeless plains of Upper Albania Danilo dragged the materials a weary day's journey from Podgoritza to Spouj. At the sight of his sufferings, and moved by the prospect of his death of torture, the people of the Zeta, who had purchased his safety, and the

Montenegrins, whose ruler he was, sent a deputation to the Pasha and implored that the life of their Bishop should be spared, and that he might be set at liberty. At the price of three thousand ducats this was promised by the Pasha. The sum was a large one for men to collect who had been deprived of all save their lives, their liberty, and their arms. They did not, however, hesitate. The people of the Zeta promised to contribute the third of the sum; Montenegro undertook to raise the remaining two-thirds. The churches gave up their plate, the women brought the silver of their girdles, the men forestalled the price of their maize and vegetables and borrowed money from the Venetian traders at Cattaro. The ransom was thus raised and duly paid, though not without precautions against further treachery, and Danilo, to the great joy of his subjects, was set at liberty.

With such an enemy it was evident no terms could be kept. The desire of revenge and the obligations of their own safety alike spurred on the Montenegrins to an act of desperation. Montenegro must be free, and must also be rendered safe from further invasion, so far at least as the lives and deaths of its people could insure its safety. In a council of the chiefs it was resolved to rid the soil of Montenegro of every renegade. The eve of the coming Christmas was fixed upon for the execution of this deed. Five brothers of the Martinovic family are said to have had the lead in this act whether of patriotic defence or of vengeance. On the night of that day the home of every renegade was entered— instant flight, death, or renunciation of the religion of Islam was proposed to him. When morning dawned not a Mussulman remained alive on the soil of Montenegro; all had either rejected the creed of the false prophet and had been baptized, had fled to the Herzegovina, or had died. Only the women and children were spared in the massacre. A ballad thus commemorates these Montenegrin vespers.

'The hallowed eve draws onward. The brothers Martinovic kindle their consecrated torches. They pray fervently to the new-born God. Each drains a cup of wine; and seizing the sacred torches, they rush forth into the darkness. Wherever there was a Turk there came the avengers. They that would not be baptized were hewn down every one. They that embraced the cross were taken as brothers before the Vladika. Gathered in Cetinje, the people hailed with songs of joy the reddening dawn of the Christmas morning: all Tzrnagora now was free.'

For a while the Turks appear to have been paralysed by this act of vigorous audacity, and made for nearly four years no direct attempt to enter Montenegro. The Montenegrins on their part made use of the time to rebuild their churches and dwelling-houses, and to prepare for that struggle which they knew to be impending. Those of the renegades who had chosen banishment rather than either death or baptism hovered along the northern frontier, and, encouraged by the presence and assistance of Turkish troops, at length entered Montenegro. They were met, attacked, and defeated. The field of battle was strewn with the slain, the rest found safety in flight or in surrender. The families of the prisoners sent to propose terms of ransom. 'You estimated the life of our Vladika,' said the Montenegrins, 'in gold, we estimate the lives of yours at what they are worth: pay us a pig for every prisoner, and they shall be sent back to you.' The insult was great to the Mussulmans, but the pigs were sent, the captives were exchanged, and this invasion was at an end.

The immediate effect of this success was of the utmost importance to Montenegro. The hardy, warlike tribes of the Berda, who occupied a territory equal in extent to that of Montenegro itself, now united themselves to the Principality for mutual defence, and, though the formal union was somewhat later, they became substantially from that moment one people with the Montenegrins. Another event of moment to the Principality was the opening of relations with Russia, then under Peter the Great, and rising to importance in the politics of Europe. This, however, was at the first of no advantage to Montenegro, for though a treaty was signed between Russia and this small Principality, these people were abandoned by Peter when he was compelled to make peace with Turkey and to give up his conquests on the Black Sea.

On the defeat of Russia the arms of Turkey were again directed towards Montenegro. Fifty thousand disciplined troops were assembled on the plain of Podgoritza for the conquest of a country which contained at most twenty thousand men, women, and children. Collecting a force less than a tenth in number of the Turkish army, the Vladika led his hasty levies suddenly against the enemy, and, falling upon them at daybreak, routed, or rather destroyed, their army. Three hundred Montenegrins were killed; of the enemy it is estimated that twenty thousand perished either on the field or in the flight.

It was evident that Montenegro was not to be subdued without efforts which would tax even the resources of Turkey in the hour of its greatest strength. The disgrace on the plain of Podgoritza must, however, be avenged by a signal overthrow of the puny antagonist. Under the Grand Vizier and Governor of Bosnia, Kiuprili, the Turks assembled on the northern frontier of Herzegovina an army of a hundred and twenty thousand men. Before, however, entering upon the campaign, Kiuprili proffered terms to Danilo, to which it appeared desirable that he should assent. To settle these terms a conference was proposed by the Turkish commander, and thirty-seven of the chiefs met him at his desire for this purpose. No sooner were they in his power than he seized and confined them, and, falling unexpectedly on the Montenegrins, bewildered with the loss of their leaders, put them to flight. Without leaders, with no ammunition, though they offered a determined resistance, yet they could not stay the march of the Ottoman general, who penetrated to Cetinje, and there hung the thirty-seven envoys whom he had enticed into his power. What the Montenegrins could not effect in a general engagement they accomplished, however, in a ceaseless series of harassing attacks, and though Kiuprili held Cetinje for a time, he purchased the advantage with the loss of nearly half his army. He revenged this loss by the devas-ation of the country. When at length he was compelled to retire through the adverse fortunes of the war in Croatia and Bosnia, and the victorious march of Prince Eugene through Hungary, it is recorded that he left not a house standing, not an altar which he had not overthrown.

From the time of this great failure to subdue the Montenegrins, from 1718 to 1737 history records only three invasions and attempts at invasion of Montenegro on the part of Turkey. Disorders at Constantinople, the murder of the Sultan Achmed III., the revolt of the janissaries, and the war with Persia, prevented the Porte from turning its arms more frequently against these people. To recount the history of these campaigns is to relate over again, with hardly a variation, the story of past invasions. In 1722 Houssen Pasha, of Trebinje, endeavoured to do what so many others had failed to achieve, and yet what Turkey was reluctant to leave undone, if by any chance it could be accomplished. Under him twenty thousand men were hurled against the northern frontier, on which Kiuprili had been for a time successful. Houssen, however, was not destined to succeed even up to the measure which the Grand Vizier had attained. He was attacked by a Montenegrin chieftain at the head of a thousand men, and for the Montenegrins to make an attack had become almost synonymous with achieving a victory. The twenty thousand men were ignominiously defeated by a force one twentieth of their own number, and their general was made prisoner.

In 1732 Topal Osman Pasha resumed the war, and with the same want of success as that which had attended Houssen Pasha. The Montenegrin annals speak of the battle on this occasion as lasting seven days, only interrupted by nightfall. At the end of the fight the remains of the Turkish army fled in disorder, abandoning tents, baggage, and artillery to the Montenegrins.

This was the last combat which took place under Danilo. Full of years, with more than a soldier's share of military exploits, amidst the regrets of his subjects, who still sing of his heroic deeds, the Vladika warrior died, in the early days of the year 1737, having recommended to the people or nominated to them as his successor his nephew Sava, who had been consecrated by the Serbian patriarch, and had acted for some years as the suffragan of the great Vladika, his uncle, and had thus relieved him in a large measure of the duties of his episcopal office.

CHAPTER XVII.

THE VLADIKAS SAVA AND VASSALI (A.D. 1735—1782).

Danilo was succeeded by a ruler of a character widely different from his own. He had in his lifetime appointed his nephew Sava as his coadjutor, and had devolved upon him the larger share of his episcopal duties, so as to allow himself to bestow greater attention to his secular duties. To this division of labour Sava seems to have readily assented, and when called to undertake the joint offices implied in the title of Prince-bishop, his temper inclined him to the ecclesiastical rather than to the civil functions of his position. His rule was marked by the emigration of the Serb patriarch, Arsenius, from Ipek, together with, it is said, 80,000 of the Christians of Old Servia. These sought a momentary refuge from Turkish oppression in Montenegro, on their way to find a permanent settlement in Austria. A detachment of warriors from Montenegro and the

Berda, aided by Albanians, safely escorted the emigrants to Nish, at that time occupied by Austrian troops.

In 1739 the Pasha of Skodra invaded the territory of the Koutchi, then in close alliance with Montenegro. Medun, the chief town of the Koutchi, was destroyed. Here however, the success of the Turks ended. Attacked by a Montenegrin force in the defiles, the Turkish army was routed with great loss. Montenegro was now blockaded by the Turks, who, mindful of past defeats, however, did not attempt to penetrate into the Principality. The blockade lasted for seven years. The army of Austria had just been defeated by the Turks, and compelled to sign the Treaty of Belgrade, and to restore to Turkey all the conquests of Prince Eugene and of the other imperial generals on the south of the Danube. Venice, unmindful of the assistance rendered by Montenegro in her past struggles with the Ottoman power, and fearing for her commercial interests, now forbade any of her subjects, under pain of death, to sell arms or powder to the Montenegrins. The strait of these people was terrible, but their spirit and resources rose with the occasion for their exercise. In accordance with the Montenegrin axiom, they sought their arsenal and magazine of powder in the lines of the enemy, and an opportune capture having replenished their stores, they sallied in great force from their homes and utterly defeated the blockading forces. In revenge for the death of the thirty-seven envoys whom Kiuprili had seized and hung in the last war, the Montenegrins avenged themselves in a way unusual to them—they burnt alive seventy of the officers whom they had captured.

The powerlessness of Austria and the hostile action of Venice in preventing supplies of ammunition reaching Montenegro, now led their Bishop to turn to Russia, which he visited in order to interest the Empress Elizabeth in the struggles of his people with the Turks. The chief result of this visit was the confirmation of the promise made by Peter the Great, but hitherto not performed, by which he undertook to pay to Montenegro the annual sum of 3,000 roubles, in compensation for the losses incurred by Montenegro through her alliance with Russia in the last war.

Sava had desired to devote himself strictly to his religious duties, and wished to escape from the turmoil both of ecclesiastical and civil life; but such a division of his offices was hardly possible under the circumstances of the country. He now resolved to find the quiet which he had long sought in vain.

Having therefore selected his nephew, the Archimandrite Vassali, as his coadjutor, and chosen, or indicated, one of the family of Radonic, of Niegush, to the people for their choice, he himself retired into a monastery, having devolved on these two the real care of the Principality, though he continued to bear the title of Prince. His rule is for this reason sometimes called a 'regency.'

The war of 1750 is marked by an incident preserved in the popular songs. Montenegro was again assailed by the Turkish troops. The attack now came from the Bosnian frontier; but, before marching, the Pasha, or Vizier, of Bosnia, sent to 'the Black Monk,' as the Turks commonly called the Vladika, and demanded the haratch, or tribute, paid by the bordering provinces of Turkey, and required at the same time that the Bishop should add an annual gift of twelve Montenegrin maidens from twelve to fifteen years of age, and should see that they were good looking. The danger was great, the array of the Pasha was a menacing one, and he had the reputation of being a successful soldier. In this strait the Vladika summoned the captains of the celos and the voivodes of the various nahias, and laid the demand before them. They waited for his word. 'He that advises compliance,' thundered forth

Vassali, 'I will instantly excommunicate.' All declared that they would never consent to terms of such ignominy as the Pasha had required. The demands of the Bosniac were answered with scorn, not to say with such a scolding as recalls the custom of Homeric heroes. 'Renegade,' was the reply of the Vladika, 'eater of the plums of the Herzegovina' —we may suppose the words were not spoken at random—' we will pay you tribute, indeed; it shall be tribute, however, not of gold, but of stones from our rocks; and, as to the twelve maidens, Montenegrin girls are not born and brought up for your service. Twelve tails from our swine to decorate your turban is all that shall be given to a renegade. Come for the tribute, and we will give you Montenegrin welcome. But, when you come, prepare to leave behind your skull. There are plenty of comrades for it among the Turkish skulls which whiten our fields.'

The confidence of the Montenegrins seemed for a time hardly justified. The Turkish forces advanced in overwhelming numbers. Powder again failed the Montenegrins, and Venice renewed the former prohibition, and warned all her subjects not to aid in any way the gallant troops of Montenegro in their dire distress. No one was to sell pistol, gun, nor powder to the mountaineers, lest Venetian commerce might chance to suffer from the vengeance of the Turk. A Serb from Cattaro, however, disregarding the interdict of the selfish republic, conveyed a store of war material into Montenegro. The supply came when the war stock was quite exhausted. The unexpectedness of the succour inspired them with fresh courage, and, making a desperate assault upon the Turkish position—as, to use the words of a Montenegrin song, a pack of wolves upon a flock of sheep—they defeated their invaders. The commander did not, however, leave his skull behind, according to the invitation of the Vladika: wounded in the action, he wisely fled from the scene of defeat and slaughter.

However brilliant the exploits of these unconquerable people might be, and though they had maintained the priceless gifts of liberty and national independence, it is not to be supposed but that they had at this period suffered greatly in these ceaseless invasions. The annals of Montenegro present a sad picture of destitution and suffering. Their printing-presses had been long destroyed, their schools were in ruins, the whole country seemed to be lapsing into the same state of barbarism as the surrounding provinces occupied by the Turks.

Hardly any one was left who could read or write, and even the priests had barely enough knowledge to allow of their repeating the offices of the church. Vassali now undertook a mission to Russia, to procure means to renew the schools, and to concert as to the civil and military organization, which had been greatly neglected. His first journey was made in 1754, and he was partially successful. This led to a second journey, in 1758, when he succeeded in obtaining a gift of 1,000 ducats from the Empress Elizabeth, and an authorization for the admission of fifteen young Montenegrins into the military academy at St. Petersburg. During a third journey, in 1765, Vassali was taken ill and died, and was buried in the church of St. Alexander Nevski, in that city.

By the death of Vassali, the real though not titular Prince of Montenegro, the rule reverted to the feeble hands of the aged Sava, who continued to preside over its destinies until his death.

Montenegro was at this time the theatre of an incident which relieves the monotony of its records of invasions and victories. In 1762 the Czar Peter III., the husband of the Empress Catherine, was murdered, and his body exposed to public view at St. Petersburg. However, as is the case with most murdered princes, a report soon spread that he had escaped from his assassins, and was at large. The report probably suggested to an adventurer the deception successfully practised upon the Montenegrin people. This was the easier to accomplish because scarcely any there had known the late Emperor. A Russian, giving himself out to be the Emperor, whose real name, according to other authorities, was Stephen the Little (Stiepan Mali), suddenly appeared on the southern confines of Montenegro. His own statement was that he had escaped from the assassins of his wife, and that he had, after many adventures, succeeded in reaching the Albanian coast. He asked to be allowed to find in Montenegro the asylum which it was always ready to offer to the distressed. As to the future, he had no desire to remount the throne of Russia; his sole ambition was to live and die for the cause of Montenegro, and to aid in reversing the disastrous day of Kossova. He thus enlisted the sympathies of the people, engaged their pride, and led captive their ambition. The Vladika Sava was at best but weak, he had long renounced the world, and was now enfeebled by old age. Stephen engrossed the business of the Principality, and spared the aged Vladka, glad to be relieved of the cares of secular life, and content that the new comer should be, for a time, the virtual, if unacknowledged, ruler of Montenegro. He was evidently a man of energy and ability, and Venice was alarmed for the quiet of her possessions and her commerce. Austria distrusted the motives of the pretender. Russia, though deeply interested, appears to have treated his claim with contempt; and this has led to the supposition that Stephen the Little was only an instrument in the hands of the Russian court, which sought by his means to obtain a footing and position in Montenegro. This, indeed, is the Turkish version of the whole incident. Whether the Turkish suspicions had any grounds or not, the presence of Stephen was made the pretext for a new invasion of the Principality, and three armies, one from the north by way of Niksic, and the other two on the southern frontier, advanced simultaneously upon Montenegro. These forces were variously estimated; one account makes them reach the number of 67,000 men, another account swells their number to 100,000. In addition to these, the Venetian troops were encamped at Budua, and menaced the Montenegrin frontier from that quarter. To oppose these armies the Montenegrins, with the allied nahias of the Berda, could only depend upon from 10,000 to 12,000 troops.

Powder again was wanting to the Montenegrins,

and resistance seemed hopeless. Suddenly the whole face of affairs was changed. On the 2nd of November—the Montenegrin annals have preserved the exact date of their deliverance—a violent thunderstorm burst over the southern frontier. A flash of lightning destroyed the Venetian magazine of powder. The thunder rolled and the lightning played with unaccustomed energy around the Turkish troops, and either dreading an explosion, or, as another account states, in consequence of a similar explosion, the Turkish troops fled. On the northern frontier the Montenegrins captured a large convoy destined for the Bosnian troops, and paralyzed by this loss—to them serious, as winter was fast approaching—this army withdrew.

The ballad which narrates the deliverance of the country from this invasion ends with a thanksgiving which reads like a verse from one of the books of Maccabees. 'Thus,' cries the Montenegrin bard, 'thus does the true God send help to them who pray to Him. Believe therefore in Christ, dear brother; believe in the God whom the Tzrnogorski adore, the God from whom they receive gladness and courage and health.'*

Though it would seem that Stephen the Little

---

* CYPRIEN ROBERT, t. i. p. 155.

had taken no part in the struggle, and doubts have even been cast upon his personal courage, yet on the withdrawal of the Turkish armies the pretender, with the concurrence, it is affirmed, of Prince Dolgorouki, the Russian envoy, was now invested with the regency on behalf of the aged Sava. In this position Stephen showed great capacity and vigour. He laboured with success in reforming the harsher features of the long border warfare. He shot all Montenegrins convicted of robbery, and instituted a police force of such efficiency, that it was said if a purse or, what was a greater temptation, a pistol lay exposed on the rocks in any part of Montenegro, no one would venture to appropriate the one or the other. Add to this he laboured in the construction of roads throughout the Principality, established courts of justice, caused a census to be made of all men able to bear arms, and, in short, proved by his capacity to rule that he could not have been Peter III.

In one way, however, Stephen the Little bore a resemblance to the unfortunate Czar whom he personated. In the midst of his labours for the good of the country which had given him an asylum and had endorsed his claims to royalty, during 1774, he was strangled in his bed by a Greek whom he had taken into his service, but who is believed to have been the emissary of the Pasha of Skodra, Mehemet Bouchatli.

His death left the government of Montenegro again in the incompetent hands of Bishop Sava. This was the signal for a fresh invasion of Turks under the same Pasha of Skodra, who is charged with procuring the assassination of Stephen Mali. This, however, like the former invasions, was repulsed by the Montenegrins, and the Turks retired, having suffered great loss. In the same year the treaty of Kainardji gave peace to Turkey and Russia, and though, as usual, no mention was made in the treaty of the Montenegrins, they had the satisfaction of knowing that their efforts and successes had prevented the Turks from sending troops from the Herzegovina and Albania to arrest the march of the Russian armies. It was the only satisfaction they had.

Sava died full of years in 1782, having been consecrated bishop-coadjutor to his uncle Danilo in 1719, to whom he succeeded in 1735. He had attained the sixty-third year of his episcopate, and the forty-seventh of his rule as Prince-bishop.

CHAPTER XVIII.

PETER I. (1782—1830.)

On the death of Sava, his great-nephew, the Archimandrite Peter Petrovic, was appointed Prince. He had been present with Vassali at the time of his death at St. Petersburg, and since the murder of Stephen the Little had assisted the aged Vladika in the government of Montenegro. On his appointment he proceeded as far as Vienna on his way to Russia for consecration. On the refusal, however, of the Russian ambassador in that city to grant him a passport to enter Russia, he made application to the Serb Patriarch at Carlowitz, and was by him consecrated in 1784. At that moment Montenegro, a prey to the intestine disorders which the feebleness of Sava had encouraged, or at least had not permitted him to repress, was menaced with a formidable Turkish invasion. The resources of the country were well-nigh exhausted, and the supplies of arms and powder had as usual failed. In this strait the new Vladika turned towards Russia, which he reached the following year, in order to obtain the necessary means of defence. He had, however, no sooner reached Russia than an order of Potemkim was handed to him directing him to quit the country in twenty-four hours.

On his return to Montenegro the Vladika found that the disorganization which reigned throughout the country menaced it with more serious evils than the Turkish armies on the frontier, and he devoted his great energies and abilities to repress the daily outrages which were perpetrated, and to restore peace and concord among his subjects.

On the breaking out of war in 1788 between Turkey and the allied forces of Austria and Russia, the Vladika was invited by the court of Vienna to join with those two powers in the war against Turkey. The tempting offer was made by Austria that the Prince of Montenegro should be reinstated in the territories held by the old princes of Zeta, and should include within his dominions Albania and the strip of land lying between Lake Skodra and the Adriatic as far as the outlet of the Bojana River, and also the Herzegovina. I need hardly remind the reader that Dalmatia was then in the possession not of

Austria but of Venice. For a time Peter hesitated to involve the country in war at the instigation of Austria; when however, these overtures were backed by the invitation of Russia, the Vladika prepared for active hostilities.

The state of things on the side of Albania was in favour of the Austrio-Russian alliance. Kara Mahmoud, the Pasha of Skodra, the direct descendant of the renegade Montenegrin Prince Stanicha, and the acknowledged leader of the powerful clan of Montenegrin Mussulmans, had made himself virtually independent of Turkish control, though still nominally a subject of the Porte. This state of semi-independence had been acknowledged, or at least had been acquiesced in, by the Turkish Government. With him Austria opened direct communications with a view to obtain his support in the war, and in order to settle the terms of co-operation sent an envoy to Skodra. Affecting to entertain the proposals, Kara Mahmoud enticed the envoy and his companions into his power, and having murdered them, forwarded their heads to Constantinople as a proof of his own fidelity.

When this murder was known, Austria endeavoured to induce the people of Montenegro to take arms. The request met with a direct refusal. They could do nothing unless directed by their own Vladika. As the intentions of Kara Mahmoud to invade Montenegro were no longer a secret, and Turkish troops were mustering on the frontier, Peter gave the order, which was joyfully obeyed by the people. The Koutchi and Pipcri, as the tribes immediately threatened by the Pasha, assembled in force, but only to find themselves without powder for the campaign. A small contingent of about four hundred men, sent by Austria, either disheartened by this want or acting under obedience to orders from Vienna, withdrew first to the inaccessible retreats of the Lovchen, and then to Cattaro, leaving the Montenegrins to carry on the war as best they could. The vigour with which the war was pressed on the Dneiper and the Danube seemed for a time to promise lasting advantages to Montenegro. Everywhere the Turks were defeated with heavy loss of men and material. These prospects, however, were suddenly clouded over. Sweden declared war with Russia. Joseph II. of Austria died, and his death soon occasioned a change of policy at the Austrain court. Russia withdrew from the war. Austria in 1791 made peace and abandoned her conquests. Worse than even this, or more galling to the Montenegrins, Austria gratuitously, in making peace, included Montenegro in the list of revolted Turkish provinces for which terms were demanded.

The four nahias of the Berda, which had for several years been virtually united to Montenegro, were now definitely incorporated into the Principality. About this date all the people of the district round Trebinje, wearied with the oppression of the Turks, emigrated to Montenegro. The refugees at first attempted to settle in the district of the Bielopavlichi, but the lands there not supplying the needs of such an increase to the inhabitants, they withdrew to the district of the Uscogues in the Upper Moratcha, where they found the means of living, and brought a considerable accession of strength to Montenegro. The territory of the Principality, though still a prey to internal division, was daily consolidating, a fact which was watched with natural jealousy by the Government of Turkey.

Kara Mahmoud collected a force of about 20,000 men on the south frontier, and prepared to penetrate into Montenegro from Podgoritza. The evident object of the threatened invasion was to hinder the union of the eight nahias which compose the present Principality. As I have mentioned in the early part of this volume, the territory of Turkey indents that of Montenegro both on the north and the south, so that the distance from Spouj on the south to Niksic on the north, both fortresses being in the possession of Turkey, is only about twelve miles. East of a line drawn from one to the other fortress lies the country known as the Berda. West are the four cantons of Montenegro. It is clear that if the Turks could have effected a lodgment at any point between Spouj and Ostrog the connection between Montenegro proper and the Berda would have been seriously weakened. As soon as the news of the advance of the Turkish troops reached Cetinje, Peter hurried to the frontier, summoning the various tribes as he passed on, and found himself in face of the advanced guard of the Turks with a handful of men who had kept up with his rapid advance; in a few hours, however, he was joined by nearly 8,000 soldiers. For several days each of the armies were content to watch the movements of the other. At length Kara Mahmoud, trusting in his great superiority, attacked the Montenegrins in the early dawn, expecting to find them off their guard. He was deceived. They were ready for the encounter, which took place at a little cluster of houses near Spouj. The Turkish forces were totally defeated, and, leaving 1,500 men on the field of battle, Mahmoud, himself wounded in the action, fled for shelter to Spouj, and finally retired across the Moratcha.

A few years later, in 1796, Mahmoud assembled a force of 30,000 and crossed the Zeta, as though about to attempt to penetrate to Cetinje. The energetic Vladika, collecting a few hundred men, left the capital, and waited only until the reinforcements which came to his assistance allowed him to offer battle to the Pasha. The Turkish troops were now powerfully aided by the Koutchi, who had sent their contingent into the camp of Mahmoud. Peter chose a favourable spot, and having divided his small force into two bodies, he placed one of these, consisting of the best marksmen, in a pass which it was necessary for the Turks to force. He directed these to distribute a number of red fez caps on the rocks, so as to deceive the Turkish commander into the belief that every Montenegrin was present, and then taking the rest of his troops, by night he reached the rear of the Turkish camp. In the morning the Turks advanced to force the pass. The resistance was vigorous, and the Montenegrin defence so well sustained, that the Turkish troops could make no impression upon the Montenegrins, posted as they were amid the the rocks. In a short time they were in confusion, when suddenly the Vladika, at the head of his other division, attacked them in the rear. The vigour and unexpectedness of the onset decided the fate of the day. The Turkish troops broke and fled, or at least attempted to fly. Nearly the whole of them perished. Kara Mahmoud was among the slain, and his head was carried in triumph to Cetinje, where it long remained as a trophy.*

The year after this battle Venice was erased from the map of Europe, and the territory of the republic was, by the treaty of Campo Formio, divided between France and Austria, the Dalmatian possessions of Venice falling for a time to the latter power, much to the discontent of the people of Cattaro and the shores of the Bocche. This arrangement brought Montenegro eventually in contact with a new enemy, disciplined after a different sort, and led by the ablest generals of France.

In 1805 Cattaro, and the coast around the strip of land formerly in the possession of Venice, and afterwards ceded to Austria, was again in the possession of France. In the general hostilities which ensued Montenegro took part with Austria and Russia. Assisted by a squadron of the latter power, the troops of the Vladika besieged and captured Castle Nuovo at the entrance to the Bocche di Cattaro. On the

* WILKINSON, vol. i. p. 489.

advance of the French troops from Ragusa, the Montenegrins attacked them near Troitsa, and, notwithstanding the artillery fire, compelled them to fall back upon Ragusa, which they besieged, and were on the point of capturing, when directions were received from Russia that all the Montenegrin conquests were to be given up to Austria, at which the Montenegrin troops retired in disgust.

Notwithstanding the efforts of Marmont and Lauriston, the French were unable to hold possession of the Dalmatian shore and subdue the Montenegrins. Even the strategy of Marmont failed before the assaults of the Montenegrins. The rage of the French at their constant defeat was exhibited in the savage revenge taken when any of these people fell into their power. The savagery was met with equal savagery on the part of the Montenegrins.

At length came the treaty of Tilsit, by which the Bocche di Cattaro was added to the dominions of the French empire. As soon, however, as war broke out with Austria and Russia, Montenegro again came to the aid of, and lent much effectual assistance to, the allies. Before hostilities commenced, Marmont, however, sought an interview with the terrible Vladika, which took place above Cattaro. There, among other accusations, the Montenegrin chieftain was reproached with the national practice of cutting off the heads of their enemies. 'We do so,' said the Vladika; 'and why not? Which is worse, that we should take off the heads of the French who are our enemies, or that the French should take off the heads of their king and of their fellow-citizens? We do so to our foes, you to your fellow-subjects.' History has not preserved the reply of the French general to the Montenegrin prince.

When peace was established for a moment between France and Montenegro, the offer was made by the Emperor Napoleon to send a consul to reside at Cetinje, and to make a road across Montenegro for the convenience of its inhabitants—and, of course, of any French troops who might wish to cross the territory of the Prince. The latter offer was declined. The border tribes were still at war with the French. They were Montenegrins by race, and, as usual, the Montenegrins,, openly or furtively, at any rate efficiently, supported their brethren. On this occasion, irritated at the success of these vexatious inroads upon the newly acquired French territory, Napoleon is said to have threatened to bathe Montenegro in blood, and make it a veritable Monte Rosso.

The threat was never fulfilled.

In 1813, when the disasters of the French army in the Moscow campaign were known, the Vladika opened communication with Sir William Hoste, who commanded the British fleet in the Adriatic, and in conjunction with him operations were conducted against the French possessions on the shores of the Bocche. Cattaro was besieged by a Montenegrin force under the command of the civil governor. Finding the fort of S. Trinita, which includes Cattaro, was in danger of being taken, the French commander withdrew, having first mined the place and prepared for its destruction. It blew up soon after the last of the French troops had withdrawn. The capture of Spagnuolo and of Castle Nuovo soon followed, and in October of that year Cattaro surrendered to a joint force of Bocchesi and Montenegrins. The whole of the shores of the Bocche were now in the hands of the Vladika, and at an assembly of the people it was resolved to unite the district with Montenegro. The English ships under Sir William Hoste, which had assisted in the reduction of Cattaro, withdrew, leaving the whole of the conquered territory in the hands of the conquerors.

Montenegro did not long remain in possession of the coveted strip of sea-coast. By an agreement between Austria and Russia the whole was seized by

Austria, and has since remained a portion of her possessions.

Relieved from the duties of war by the treaty of Vienna, and for awhile by the exhaustion of the Turks, the Vladika was now enabled to turn his attention to the domestic affairs of the country. Notwithstanding all his endeavours, the internal affairs of Montenegro were extremely unsatisfactory. Want had gone on almost to famine. Worse than this, broils and strife prevailed throughout the country. Dissension had grown into disorganization. Village was arrayed against village, as well as province against province. Many families, despairing of repose, emigrated from their native country. Many of these went to Servia, some to Russia. The common enemy, taking advantage of these untoward circumstances, again invaded Montenegro. An army of 12,000 men entered the Principality, sacking and burning the villages on the frontier. This invasion partook more of a border raid on a large scale than of regular war. It was repelled with the loss of 1,500 of the enemy. Large booty and a number of horses became the prize of the conquerors, together with a number of prisoners, many of whom the exasperated Montenegrins decapitated amid the yet burning ruins of their villages.

Then ensued an unusually long period of peace. From 1821 to 1830 the troubles which had arisen in Greece and Moldo-Wallachia sufficiently engaged the attentions of the Turks, and prevented their undertaking any formal invasion of Montenegro during these ten years. On the part of the Montenegrins, however, this time was marked by perpetual forays into the Turkish provinces, in order to procure the subsistence which their impoverished and desolated country could no longer yield to them. Their necessities were the greater because, from 1814 till 1825, the annual payment first made by Peter the Great of Russia as compensation for their losses as the allies of that power had been withheld by the Emperor Alexander. This payment was, however, resumed in the latter year, and has since been paid with regularity.

This period of cessation from war, if not of repose, was employed by the Vladika Peter in stringent measures to remedy the disorders which had grown up within the country. The limits between Austria and Montenegro were now settled, the border raids were checked, the vendetta successfully repressed, and a great step made towards the amelioration of the condition of Montenegro by the rigid application of the code of laws promulgated by the Vladika in

1796. The severity with which he visited any breach of these laws is still a tradition of the country over which he ruled so long and with so great advantage to his people. They reverenced him as a father, he treated them as his children, and did not spare the rod in their correction.

As the history of his reign and his conduct in the wars with Turkey and afterwards with France sufficiently witness, he was a man of iron will and of dauntless bravery; but, more than this, his administrative abilities were considerable; he possessed the art of influencing others; he had the gift of great eloquence. His energy in war and his activity in the government of the country were in striking contrast to the gentleness of his disposition. In his personal habits he was simple even to austerity, so much so that in his last illness he had not even a fire within the four bare walls which served him for a bedroom.

His end was characteristic. In October, 1830, the heads of the various plemena had assembled in Cetinje to discuss the best means for the settlement of the differences which still existed in several parts of the united Principality. Gathered around the fire in the ample apartment which served as the Vladika's kitchen and the senate house of the people, the Vladika, whilst addressing the senators and others whom he had summoned, was seized with a fainting fit. He was removed to his bed-chamber, and thither, when sufficiently recovered, he called the assembled chiefs, dictated his will, and received from them the promise of obedience to his wishes as expressed in this his last testament, and then amid the prayers of his subjects he commended his soul to God, and quietly expired in the eighty-first year of his age and the forty-eighth of his rule.

An annual feast day and a pilgrimage to his coffin at Cetinje, which is attended by large numbers of Serbs, not only in Montenegro but beyond its frontier, perpetuate the memory of the great Vladika and saint, Peter I.

CHAPTER XIX.

PETER II. (1830—1851).

THE task which had engaged the last thoughts of the great Vladika was not intermitted by his death. By his will, which the assembled chiefs had promised to obey, and to which, without such promise, the reverence entertained by them for their Prince would have ensured a ready obedience, enjoined upon them to promote by every means within their power the concord of all classes in Montenegro. In this will he urged them to discourage the reprisals and acts of revenge which so fatally disturbed the peace of their common country, and that he might assist them in commencing this great work he called upon them to swear to abstain from all deeds of personal hostility until St. George's day in the coming year.

Around the coffin of the Vladika whom they had

so often followed to the field the chiefs swore to observe these his last injunctions.

This done, they prepared for the funeral, and, amid the tears of the whole people, carried his coffin to the little chapel of the convent. There he lies, coffined but unburied, the object still of the affectionate reverence of the Montenegrin people. At the urgent entreaties of his children, his subjects, his successor proclaimed his canonization; and St. Peter Petrovic at this day divides with St. Elias and St. George the honours paid in Montenegro to the saints of God.

Though no formal instrument had given to the Vladika the right of nominating his successor, yet he was permitted to do this, and by his last will Peter I. named his nephew, Radatamova, to the office of Prince and Bishop of Montenegro. The young man shrank from the post. He refused for a time the honour. His desire indeed had been to fit himself for a military life. His literary tastes also led him to wish to avoid the life of active toil and self-denial which the proferred post demanded. Add to this, he was but seventeen years of age. His disinclination did not divert the chiefs from their choice, and at length he consented to obey the wishes of his deceased uncle. It was fortunate for

Montenegro that he did so. Of course at this age he had not been set apart for the ecclesiastical life. Notwithstanding this, on the day after his uncle's death, the assembled chiefs of the various plemena vested him in ecclesiastical costume, placed in his hand the pastoral staff, and presented him to the people as their future ruler.

A slight opposition was manifested to his succession. It was natural that this should be the case. This, however, was speedily repressed, and among the first persons who pressed around to offer him their homage were the Archimandrite of Ostrog and the civil governor, Vuk Radovic, the representatives of the ecclesiastical and secular authority of the Principality.

A short time after his accession to power the Bishop of Prisrend was invited to ordain the new Prince. In the little chapel of Our Lady in the Island of Kom, on the Lake of Skodra, the young Prince was advanced to the offices of deacon and priest, and invested with all ecclesiastical rights and duties entrusted to and enjoined upon an archimandrite.

Three years after his ordination the new Prince made a journey to St. Petersburg, and was there consecrated to the episcopal office, and took the name of Peter in honour of his deceased uncle. The year before such consecration (1832) was, however, made memorable in Montenegrin history by two events.

At the time of the death of Kara Mahmoud, Pasha of Skodra, Albania had become virtually independent of the Sultan, though still owning a nominal subjection to his government. His son, Moustapha Boutchali, was less able or less fortunate than his father, and was compelled by the Grand Vizier, Mahmoud Reschid, to recognise the authority of the Porte. He had no sooner succeeded in this than the Grand Vizier turned his attention to Montenegro, and offered substantial advantages to the people and to their Prince if they would acknowledge the suzerainty of the Sultan. An extended territory and a concession of hereditary right to rule was to be given to the Prince, in the same way that it had been just given to Serbia. The conditions of the two Principalities were, however, essentially different. Serbia had for a long period been a province of Turkey. Montenegro had always asserted, and had made good its assertion, to independence. Peter refused the offer of the Grand Vizier. On this refusal a Turkish force, the advanced guard of a larger force to follow, was directed against Montenegro. So sudden was the attack, that the first intimation of the invasion was the appearance of a small army of 7,000 men on the frontier near Spouj. These troops invaded the Montenegrin territory at Martinic, the scene of a desperate engagement in the time of the late Vladika. The attack might have been in some measure successful but for the bravery and self-devotion of the village priest. Assembling his parishioners, he resisted the Turkish force, and succeeded in delaying their advance, and though he laid down his life in accomplishing this, yet the delay allowed the armed levies of the Bielopavlic and of the Piperi to assemble. The Turks were driven back over the Moratcha with great slaughter—the invasion was at an end.

The other event which happened in the same year was of a different character. The civil governor, which office had come to be regarded, like that of the Vladika, as an hereditary right, and was always bestowed upon one of the Radovic family of Niegush, though he had been one of the first to render homage to the Bishop, had resented his election. He was now accused of a design to place Montenegro under the control or suzerainty of Austria. What were the proofs of the charge we are not informed. That he was plotting the overthrow of the Vladika there can be little doubt.* He was banished, and the office of civil governor, which in the time of the energetic Peter I. had been stripped of most of its importance, was now formally abolished.

Up to this time, though the late Vladika had promulgated a code of laws, he had not succeeded in establishing respect for these laws. The sturdy independence of the chieftains refused to obey their requirements, without, however, contesting the authority of the lawgiver. Laws were alien to the Principality, which had been governed—so far as it could be said to be governed—by old, unwritten, and variously interpreted customs. The present Vladika enforced obedience with salutary rigour. In his visitation of his diocese he threatened the refractory with excommunication, and punished with the secular arm those who violated the laws. Up to this time revenge for the death of a Montenegrin was so deeply impressed upon all the members of the community as a sacred duty, that the execution of the sentence of the law often led to bitter feuds and blood-shedding between the pleme of the criminal and that to which the executioner

* WILKINSON, vol. ii. p. 461.

belonged. To prevent the indulgence of this passion the Vladika condemned the criminal to be shot, and caused a selection of men from various plemena to be made, who fired at the same instant, and so prevented the possibility of any one person being responsible for carrying out the sentence of the law. Every form of the vendetta was severely repressed. Theft was trampled out. The quarrels which existed, and led oftentimes to bloodshed, between the different plemena of the Principality, were sternly punished. National customs and national habits were not allowed to stand in the way of the laws. Time-honoured practices, such as raids and cattle-lifting, were no longer permitted, and even the custom of cutting off the heads of the slain and preserving them as public trophies was made illegal, and in a great measure abolished, by the exertions of the Vladika. In all parts of the Principality, between the rigour of his acts and the respect felt for his commands, a great improvement was effected in the political and social life of the Montenegrins before his death.

According to the very competent evidence of an eye-witness of these improvements—'Until the late reforms the power of the Vladika was more limited, being rather a moral influence than an actual jurisdiction. He had no right to punish any one for the greatest crimes; and though he might interpose his episcopal authority and threaten with excommunication, his commands might be defied; and he was obeyed rather out of respect for his holy office, for his superior understanding, and from a belief that he acted from just and wise motives. In the absence of laws, every one defended his own cause by force; none were amenable to justice, and none were deterred by fear of punishment which none had the right to inflict. Blood was avenged by blood, and the *lex talionis* was carried out much in the same way as among other people in a primitive state of society. If the murderer had left the country, their vengeance fell on his nearest relation. He in turn found new avengers; and sometimes whole villages made war in this way, so that neither governor nor Vladika could stop the effusion of blood. Families were obliged to avenge the violent deaths that happened in their villages, and villages, or even whole districts, to take the part of their inhabitants against those of another village or district. Truces were sometimes established between the hostile parties, as, for instance, when they had common or adjoining fields to cultivate. In cases where one party stood more in need of the truce than the opposite one, it must pay for it; and the attack of the foreign enemy alone established a general truce for all private hostilities.' *

The contrast between the past and the present condition of Montenegro is the best testimony to the abilities and patriotism of Peter II.

The office from which he had shrunk proved no light one to the conscientious Vladika. In the moment of danger, at the alarm of the invasion of the Turks, Peter approved himself an able and intrepid captain. When the duties of his military command permitted, he was the laborious priest and eloquent preacher, to whom his people flocked for advice and instruction; and when these failed to keep his people in the right way, he sat under the shade of the tree of justice, heard their complaints, adjusted their differences, and condemned the criminal. These multiform duties he lightened by literary pursuits, and by indulging his hereditary genius for poetry. He was thus at once the leader of his people in war, their priest and bishop in peace, their instructor, their judge, and the bard to whose poems they listened, and still listen, with delight.

The solitude of the Black Mountain, together with the absence of congenial society, were felt

* WILKINSON, vol. i. p. 456.

deeply by the Vladika; but he bravely resisted all temptations to a life of ease. He was a man not only remarkable even among these men of large stature for his height, which reached six feet eight inches, and for his skill with the rifle, in which he excelled, but also for his mental accomplishments. He spoke and wrote German, Italian, French, and Russian, and found time amid the pressure of his many duties to correspond with the various literary societies of Slavonia and other lands.*

He died, after a short illness, in October, 1851, at the early age of thirty-nine years, and, according to his request, his body lies entombed in a mortuary chapel, for which he had provided the funds, on the top of the Lovchen Mountain.

* 'Besides his talents as a governor, the Vladika has the merit of being a distinguished Servian or Slavonian poet; and he unites all the qualities of a good soldier and an able diplomatist. He is also a member of several learned societies of Europe.'—WILKINSON, vol. ii. p. 471.

CHAPTER XX.

RESTORATION OF THE SECULAR RULE—DANILO II.

LIKE his predecessor, Peter I., the last public care of the dying Vladika had been to summon the chiefs of the various districts to Cetinje, and make known to them his dying commands. In a short address he informed them that he had by his last will appointed Danilo, son of his brother Stanko, to succeed him, and that, in order to fit him for this post, he had sent him abroad for his education, and he added, 'I bequeath my curse to every one who does not honour and obey this my last will, which I direct you to read to all the people, solemnly assembled for that purpose.' The following morning, the 18th of October, 1851, he died, after a reign of twenty-one years.

Immediately after his death the chiefs present and others assembled at a solemn skuptchina, or council, at Cetinje. Here the will of the Vladika was read to the chiefs, and by them made known to the people of the various districts which they represented.

Danilo, at that time twenty-three years of age, was the youngest son of Stanko Petrovic. He was at Vienna when the death of his uncle took place. He immediately returned to Montenegro. He came to find his right of succession disputed. His uncle Pero, brother of the late Vladika, and President of the Senate, had already won over the chiefs to support his own elevation to the dignity of Prince, and was prepared to resist the appointment of Danilo. For a time it seemed that he would be successful in his usurpation. The prudence and patience of the young Prince, however, and the influence which the known wishes of the deceased Vladika exercised over the Montenegrin people, frustrated these intrigues, and soon after his arrival at Cetinje Danilo was recognised as the successor of his uncle, Peter II.

The President and Vice-President of the Senate, as well as their chief adherents, resigned their offices, but were reinstated in them by the young Prince.

The inconveniences of the ecclesiastical rule, the need and yet danger of a divided authority, of a prince-bishop and a civil governor subordinate to him, both of which had been recognised, formerly by the long existence of that office, and now by its recent abolition, were fully comprehended by Danilo. Add to this, he was personally averse to entering the ecclesiastical state, and left Cetinje on his way to St. Petersburg meditating on the means to separate for the future the functions of the prince and the bishop. With the exception of the handful of influential chiefs who had endeavoured to prevent the sucession of Danilo, the people of Montenegro were prepared to acquiesce in the change. A skuptchina was summoned to consider the proposal which the Prince had caused to be laid before it in his absence, and, after some discussion, the fundamental articles of the constitution of Montenegro were declared to be:—

(1.) That Montenegro is a secular state, with the hereditary government of a prince.

(2.) The illustrious Danilo Petrovic is acknowledged and recognised as Prince. After his death the succession shall ever belong to the male line of his family, in order of primogeniture. On the failure of direct succession the power shall pass to his nearest relation. Should there be more than one of the same relationship, then the eldest shall succeed.

(3.) The archbishop or bishop who shall exercise the oversight of ecclesiastical affairs shall be chosen from the family of Niegush—that is, the Petrovic family—or from one of the other principal families in the country.

(4.) The organic law, the legislative acts, and customs which have hitherto served as rules for the government of the country, shall continue to be in force, save and except in the case of such as may be altered by this decree.

(5.) His Highness the Prince is invited to return as speedily as may be to his country, to make known his wishes, and to proceed, in conjunction with the Senate, to execute the same.

(6.) Commissioners extraordinary shall be immediately sent to make known the present decree to Prince Danilo and also to the Emperor of Russia.

Though Prince Danilo had, for public reasons, urged the secularization of the government of the Principality, he was now further stimulated by a private motive to carry out the contemplated change. At Trieste he met with a young, accomplished, and patriotic Serb lady, whom he afterwards married—Darinka, daughter of a wealthy merchant of that city, Marko Kochoic.

Having obtained the acquiescence of the Emperor

Nicholas of Russia to the future separation of the civil and ecclesiastical offices, Danilo returned to Montenegro.

The Porte viewed the change with disapproval. That these should have been carried out without seeking the support of Turkey was a direct assertion that Montenegro was independent of that power, and acknowledged no suzerainty in it. The hostility of Turkey led to a declaration of war, and Omar Pasha was directed to invade Montenegro. On the part of the Montenegrins the war commenced with the surprise and seizure of Jablac on the south-western frontier of the Principality. The war itself was for a time unattended with any decisive success on either part, until by a night attack, a few days after Christmas, 1852, the camp of Omar Pasha was destroyed, seventeen standards captured, and a large part of the Turks slain. On this reverse Omar Pasha changed the direction of his attack, and endeavoured to penetrate Montenegro from the northern frontier. He found this quarter guarded as watchfully and energetically as the opposite quarter. And on his advance from Grahova to Ostrog, he was met by the Prince himself, at the head of a Montenegrin corps, and was totally defeated, with great slaughter. On this he retired from the Herzegovina. No sooner had he done so, than his active opponent joined his troops on the opposite frontier, and compelled the Turks to fall back from the banks of the Zeta, when, at the mediation of Austria, the Porte made peace with Montenegro, and received from the hands of the Prince 900 prisoners who had been kept at Cetinje. The Turks lost in this war 4,500 men on the fields of battle, beside those who died in the military hospitals, either of their wounds or from disease.

In the war between Russia and Turkey assisted by England, France and Italy, Montenegro retained an attitude of neutrality, somewhat to the danger of the popularity of Prince Danilo with his subjects. This was increased by the severe measures taken by him to repress all forays upon the Turkish frontier. These he forbade by proclamation, and when this appeared insufficient, by the punishment of the offenders. It was hard to eradicate the feeling that reprisals such as these were lawful and right. The Turks were ceaselessly invading the land of the Montenegrins, and now the Prince had forbidden them to harrass their turbulent neighbours, who had forcibly taken possession of the lands which belonged to the people of Montenegro.

The nahias of the Berda were profoundly agitated on this question. The warlike Piperi, the Koutchi, who, in addition to this grievance, were Roman Catholics, with but a slight attachment to the Vladika of Montenegro, and the Bielopavlichi, who were the first to suffer when the armies of Turkey were invading the Principality, flew to arms, and proclaimed their separation from Montenegro proper. The insurrection was suppressed, but the determination of Prince Danilo that no more forays should be permitted upon Turkey severely tried the loyalty of his people. The Prince, however, persisted in the course on which he had deliberately entered.

As soon as this insurrection was suppressed, and the Prince was at leisure to turn for a moment from public occupations, he was married to Darinka Kochoic, to whom he had been betrothed nearly three years before. At a skuptchina summoned for that purpose, in the same year (1855), the new code of laws prepared by the Prince was presented for acceptance. This, though based on that promulgated by Peter I., contained many provisions on matters not contemplated by the code of his predecessor. At the same assembly a decree was passed to regulate the succession to supreme power, and his nephew, Nicholas Petrovic, then a lad of fourteen, was recognised as heir, in default of sons living at the death of Danilo. Nicholas was son of Mirko, the elder brother of Prince Danilo.

In order that he might be fitted for the post to which he might be hereafter called, Nicholas was sent to Paris to complete his education.

The discontent caused along the border by the vigorous suppression of the raids which the Montenegrins had been accustomed to make upon the Turks led to an insurrection, which, though soon repressed by the vigour of Mirko, the brother of the Prince, bore fruit afterwards in the withdrawal of the Koutchi from their allegiance.

At the end of 1856 Prince Danilo addressed to the great powers a memorial claiming on behalf of Montenegro, first, the official recognition of its independence, which, though a fact, was sometimes contested by the Porte; secondly, the extension of the frontier line both on the side of the Herzegovina and on that of Albania, so as to obviate the inconvenience to the country by the deep indentation of Turkish territory on either side; thirdly, the delineation of the frontier where Montenegro was bounded by Turkey, in the same way as it had been determined on the Austrian frontier; fourthly, the re-union of Antivari with

Montenegro, so as to allow of the inhabitants of the Principality obtaining access to the sea, for the exportation of their own productions as well as for the free importation of the produce of other countries. These four demands were presented to the Porte by envoys accredited by the Prince. Instead of complying with these demands the Porte replied by requiring the Prince to acknowledge the supremacy of the Sultan, and promised, on condition that this was done, to make over to the Prince the portion of territory to which he had laid claim on the side of the Herzegovina, the Prince undertaking, on his part, to pay to the Government of Turkey the tithes of the portion so assigned; the Sultan promised, moreover, that then he would assign to the Prince a civil list and a Turkish title, and would give the Montenegrins access to any of the Turkish ports.

These proposals of Turkey caused the intensest indignation in Montenegro, and the utmost surprise and discontent were excited by the news that the Prince was willing to acknowledge the suzerainty of the Porte on condition of his people receiving certain substantial advantages. This unexpected resolve of the Prince for a while caused him great unpopularity.

War, however, with Turkey prevented any further

consideration of this subject. This time the storm burst on the frontier of Herzegovina, at the point where the Austrian territory touches that of Turkey and of Montenegro. The Turkish troops were pushed forward from Trebinje with orders to occupy the valley of Grahova. Seven thousand men under Hussein Pasha taking the road for Klobuk, reached the plateau of Grahovatz and encamped there. The only Montenegrin force opposed to them was a small contingent of 400 men. On the news of the invasion Mirko hurried to the point which was menaced in order to assume the command of this small body. On his arrival he dispatched the Prince's secretary, Delarue, to remonstrate with the Pasha at this unprovoked invasion. On his arrival in the Turkish camp he was seized and detained as a hostage. Finding, however, that the Montenegrin troops were posted on ground which offered great difficulties in the way of the attacking forces, and that the various contingents were hourly hastening to the post of danger and ranging themselves under the command of Mirko, the Turkish commander determined to fall back from the ground which he occupied. The retreat commenced in good order. Mirko, however, who had already divined that the Turkish forces would be compelled to retreat, refusing to give way to the entreaties of his men, who burned to attack the Turkish troops, had the evening before directed the contingent of 400 men who had at the first opposed the advance of the Turkish commander to march to the rear of the enemy, and ordered its leader to post himself across the only line open for the retreat of Hussein Pasha. No sooner had the retreat of the Turkish troops commenced than the main body of the Montenegrins were seen crossing the heights along their line of march, and almost as soon as they were seen the battle commenced. A few rounds from their rifles were fired, when, throwing them aside, the Montenegrins rushed, yataghan in hand, helter-skelter upon the Turks. Before the Turkish commander could form his line of battle his troops broke and fled, but only to fall under the swords of the mountaineers. In vain two battalions of the Imperial Guard attempted by their firmness to arrest the advance of the Montenegrins. In vain the artillery, of which the Montenegrins were destitute, scattered death into the ranks as they advanced to the attack. The artillerymen were shot down at their posts, and the artillery was speedily silenced. For two hours the fight and flight had continued under these circumstances, when a short sharp rifle fire in their front told the

Ottoman troops that their retreat itself was cut off. One division of veteran Turkish soldiers thrown into a square attempted to arrest the Montenegrins. The attempt only insured their slaughter. The Montenegrins, seizing the bayonet with one hand, dealt death with the yataghan in the other. The Turkish troops, according to the testimony of their enemies, behaved with great bravery, but all in vain. The Pasha who commanded these troops was slain, and his men perished, each one in the ranks with their commander. The resistance, however, which was offered by a portion of the Turkish force enabled many of the troops to save themselves by flight. The main part of the army, however, under Hussein Pasha, were strewn along the plain of Grahova. The Montenegrin loss was 400 men. Of the Turks 2,237 corpses were counted on the plateau of Grahovatz, and their whole loss before reaching a place of safety amounted to 4,000; in addition to this the whole of their artillery, military stores, and standards fell into the hands of the victors. Well might these wonder at the completeness of their victory. The expression of their wonder broke out in utterances which breathe the spirit of Hebrew poetry, and the Montenegrin song which recounts the events of the battle thus concludes: 'Dear God, the miracle of our victory is the work of thine omnipotence. Thine, dear Lord, be the glory of all the works of thine hands.'

The victory of the Montenegrins at Grahova was revenged by the fugitives upon the peasants of the Herzegovina, who it was known could not fail to rejoice at the defeat of the Turks. The news of this victory was carried to the farthest east, and increased the respect which was entertained for the Montenegrin name, whilst Grahova itself has from that day become a part of the territory ruled over by the Prince of Montenegro.

According to the request of the Prince, the great powers of Europe joined in marking out the limits of Montenegro and deciding upon its future boundaries. No rectification of the frontier has, however, followed upon the labours of this commission. Their frontier remained as open to attack as before, and no port was granted to them as an outlet for their commerce. During the next year no event of importance took place in Montenegro, and the Prince was fully occupied in carrying out the scheme for the social reformation of his people. The new code was enforced in all its parts, and the people, however at the first they might have been averse to the novelties which it sanctioned or enjoined, recognised the patriotism and wisdom of their Prince in the various actions of his government. The end, however, was near at hand.

In July, 1860, Prince Danilo left Cetinje for the baths at Persano on the Boche di Cattaro. After a residence of several weeks there, and whilst at Cattaro enjoying an evening walk on the promenade with the Princess on the 13th of August, he was shot by an exiled Montenegrin who had arrived in that city the day before in disguise. Danilo died the next day, and his assassin, having been tried, was hung without revealing the motives for the murder of the Prince. Attended by his young widow, the body was borne up the great pass, and was buried in the chapel re-erected by the Prince and Princess in memory of their marriage a short time before. If any expectation existed that the death of the Prince would effect any change in the Montenegrin succession, this was frustrated by the prompt action of the Princess Darinka, who, in conformity with the decree which had settled the succession, proclaimed the son of Mirko as Nicholas I., Prince of Montenegro and the Berda. Prince Danilo left behind only an infant daughter, Olga.

CHAPTER XXI.

NICHOLAS I. (1860).

I HAVE no intention of attempting to review the history of the seventeen years during which Prince Nicholas has directed the affairs of Montenegro. They have been most momentous years in the life of the nation; but the ruler is alive, and I shrink from the expression of my judgment upon the acts of his reign.

*   *   *   *   *

The order of succession made during the lifetime of the late Prince had named Nicholas the son of Mirko, elder brother of Prince Danilo, as his heir. The practice in the selection of a prince had never followed the rules applicable to the descent of landed property. Fitness, not birth, was the one consideration in the eyes of prince and people; and though neither contemplated that the succession would devolve on so young a prince, and some misgivings were naturally felt and freely expressed that he might prove unequal to the task, yet these have been forgotten in his successful rule.*

Mirko had thus been destined to see any birth-claims which he might seem to have possessed postponed in 1851 to the intellectual claims of his younger brother; while, in 1860, he saw himself again passed over, and his son selected to be the ruler of Montenegro. On both occasions he appears to have acquiesced loyally in the choice by which he was thrust aside. Only this acquiescence preserved peace to Montenegro. No one within its bounds was more popular, no one more calculated to secure the popular suffrage than the Grand Voivode Mirko. A fiery paladin, the very *beau-idéal* of Montenegrin chivalry, he was the trusted leader in every campaign, and his exploits and the exploits of those whom he commanded at Grahova are still favourite subjects for the evening conversation in the cottage homes throughout Montenegro. His presence, it was believed, would secure victory to the troops whenever he might be called to command

---

* Prince Nicholas was born 13th September, 1840 (O.S.), married 10th September, 1860 (O.S.), to Milena, daughter of Peter Voukotic, and has one son, Danilo Alexander, and six daughters.

them. His deeds of bravery sound more like those of the Homeric heroes than of a nineteenth-century soldier. His exploit at Ostrog when he foiled the Turkish army and withdrew, without giving them any advantage during his retreat, reads like a tale of romance. His victories carry us back to the days of Montrose or of Charles Edward. Yet he was not a mere fiery chieftain. He laboured with patient industry in the reorganization of the forces, and in adapting their tactics to the new requirements of the times. His experiments in rice and coffee, and his labours to render the rocks around Rjeka productive, give us a picture of a scientific agriculturist. A volume of the poems which he printed shows that the gift of song, hereditary in his family, was cultivated by him with success. The abnegation of such a man was remarkable, more remarkable indeed than his military skill, sagacity, and fierce courage.

Mirko died of cholera in 1865, and lies buried by the side of the Great Vladika, Peter I., in the same church where his brother Danilo had been buried five years before.

Of Prince Nicholas, a recent writer thus speaks:—

'In appearance the Prince is tall and remarkably

handsome; his hair is black, he wears both beard and moustaches, contrary to the fashion of his country, where only the latter are worn, often of immense size and length. With a commanding appearance, he still has a most benevolent expression of countenance, due to the softness of a very fine pair of eyes, and his manners are most captivating. He is very dignified, but at the same time most kind, without being in the least patronising; and I was told by those who know him best that he has a most equable temper, and that an angry word seldom was heard from him.' *

Add to this, however brave and skilful in war, his tastes are those of peace. His delight is in the schools which he has planted throughout Montenegro, in his farm, in his collection of antiquities, and his study. Like his predecessor, he belongs to the class of 'royal and noble authors,' and his songs circulate from the northern extremity of Herzegovina to Skodra. Over this tract of country he rules, if not by right of territory, yet by the gifts of personal influence, over hearts, if not over lands. To him disputants in the Herzegovina submit their differences. In him the hopes of the inhabitants of the whole of the Zeta and of lands

* *Rambles in Istria*, &c., p. 225.

beyond the boundaries of the old principality of Montenegro yet centre, whilst his people obey him implicitly as they would obey a father whom they love. If he has at any moment tried the loyalty of his subjects, it has been when the moderation and self-restraint of his dealings with Turkey have conflicted with the fiery impatience of the Montenegrins at the rejection of their fair demands. Yet even then they have in the end dutifully acquiesced in his wisdom, and have acknowledged that "Nikita" knew what was best, even though they were unable to sympathize with his moderation. Such a Prince is worthy of a larger sphere of usefulness, and if his life be spared amid the dangers of the battle-field, this part of Turkey may yet find in Prince Nicholas Petrovic one who is able to heal its wounds and restore to it its long-forgotten peace and prosperity.

THE END.

PRINTED BY VIRTUE AND CO., LIMITED, CITY ROAD, LONDON.

www.ingramcontent.com/pod-product-compliance
Lightning Source LLC
Chambersburg PA
CBHW032043230426
43672CB00009B/1448